RAISING REBELS

PARENTING ADVICE FROM THE GIRL YOUR PARENTS WARNED YOU ABOUT

DAYNA MARTIN

ISBN: 978-0-6484303-2-2 (Paperback)

ISBN: 978-0-6484303-3-9 (Ebook)

www.turnerbooks.com.au

This book is dedicated to Leif Cid, for the undying support and love through this sacred journey with our children, and the children of the world.

CONTENTS

FOREWORD

NANCI NOTT

rebel

noun

a person who rejects the rules, authority, or cultural norms of the society in which they live.

verb

to react against something.

The word *rebel* has negative connotations to some people, because we live in a society that values conformity and obedience, above freedom and mutual respect.

Schools don't want rebels. Institutions don't want rebels. Governments don't want rebels. Yet, if someone were to call me a rebel, I would consider it a compliment. Why?

When my oldest daughter was born, almost two decades ago, I swore never to forget the magic inherent in her existence, and promised her a lifetime of unconditional love and acceptance. I think we all make similar promises to our newborns.

The thing is, the nature of parenthood is something we can't begin to understand until we find ourselves in the midst of it... and we *all* begin as novices.

There is no such thing as a *perfect parent*. We learn, alongside our children, all the time. As our children grow, so do we, and each new stage of life throws us into uncharted territory. Like childhood, parenthood is a unique exploration of the meaning of life.

It is natural to seek guidance on this journey. Unfortunately, most of the accepted parenting pedagogy works *against* the best interests of families. Much of the damage done to children in our society is inflicted as a direct result of our cultural ideation of what it means to be a *good parent*. In our efforts to keep those heartfelt promises to our newborns, we break them.

Early in my parenting life, I decided I didn't agree with most of the advice I was given, or any of the books at my disposal. *Crying it out* seemed cruel. *Discipline* felt unnecessary. *Setting limits* didn't sit well with my instincts.

My daughter had a cot, which we never used. She breastfed well into her toddler years. She ate when she was hungry, slept when she was tired, and we went everywhere together. I received a lot of judgement as a result of my parenting methods, especially in the beginning.

My daughter and I played games, read books, travelled, and shared a host of real life experiences – some positive, some not-so-positive.

I was by no means a perfect parent, because no one ever is. But my connection with my daughter was strong, and based on trust. We knew that, no matter what life had in store for us, we had genuine love and acceptance for one another.

When the time came for my daughter to start school, I balked. It seemed unnatural to palm her off to strangers, who couldn't possibly love her, or care for her, in the way she deserved. I didn't want my daughter's inherent kindness, enthusiasm, and individuality bled dry from her sensitive psyche.

By the age of five, she was reading novels, because life is the best teacher. There was no way I was going to miss her for six hours a day, just so she could be 'taught' the letters of the alphabet.

I thought back upon my own school experiences, and knew I didn't want that life for my daughter.

I kept the promise I made to my newborn, all those years ago, by choosing *not* to send her to school. It was the best decision I ever made.

Seventeen years and three kids later, I'm more convinced than ever – society has it all wrong.

We should not be conditioning our children to obey authority.

We should be raising rebels, capable of cultivating their own authority, over their own lives, in their own ways.

My children are compassionate, free-thinking, self-motivated individuals, who are intrinsically motivated to learn, grow, and give of themselves to others.

My children are secure in the knowledge that if I can provide something for them, I will – with no conditions attached. For this reason, my children are generous, and undemanding.

My children know that I value their opinions. For this reason, whinging is not an issue for us.

My children know I will give them my attention

when they require it. For this reason, they aren't disruptive.

My children have always been allowed to make their own choices when it comes to food, sleep, hygiene, clothing, and how they spend their time. For these reasons, they have learned to make healthy decisions for themselves – no power struggles necessary.

And yet, society tells us to micromanage every aspect of our children's lives. To deny their self-responsibility. To dictate what they do (and don't) learn. Society tells children to obey, without question. This makes no sense to me. Mainstream parenting feels illogical, counterintuitive, and cruel.

The world has changed a lot since my oldest daughter was born. The internet enables us to access a wider variety of information, and helps us find like-minded people we might never have encountered, were it not for being globally connected. But it hasn't always been this way.

In the early two-thousands, I felt an invisible barrier separating my family from the rest of the world. I never doubted my convictions, because I never doubted my children. But living by principles nobody else seemed to share was an (unsurprisingly) isolating experience.

About ten years ago, I discovered Dayna Martin online, and realised there were *other people in the world who lived like us.* That realisation gave me hope, and assisted in eliminating any remnants of subconscious self-doubt lurking beneath the surface of my surety. I know this book will bring similar comfort to countless others.

It's okay to walk a solitary path, but it helps to know there are supportive voices to counteract the constant stream of culturally-inculcated criticism. I don't want other parents to feel alone, especially those whose stubbornness might not outweigh self-doubt in the face of judgement; for whom that feeling of isolation is most damaging.

I have so much love for this book, because I know first-hand how important it can be to find parenting literature more in line with what we know to be true.

So much has changed since I was a new parent. Society is waking up. Our global community is teeming with families who live life like we do – with freedom and respect. There is no shortage of support for those who seek it, especially if you know where to look.

My oldest daughter, Xanthe – the child who bore

the brunt of me finding my feet as a parent – is now a young woman, and my best friend.

Xanthe has many passions, and is always looking for proactive ways to support others. In fact, she published the book you are currently reading, as her own not-for-profit contribution to a cause she sincerely believes in. Xanthe is artistic, intelligent, ethical, generous, gentle, and intensely compassionate. When I grow up, I hope to be just like my daughter.

Raising our children is the most revolutionary act we are likely to accomplish in our lifetime. Our actions, thoughts, and behaviours shape our children's environments. We have a responsibility to nurture, guide, and protect our children. But we also need to give our kids the space to shape their own lives. Parents are collectively responsible for the generational legacies we – and our children – leave behind.

Can you imagine a world predominantly populated by peaceful, passionate, freethinking, change-makers? Can you picture a society characterised by integrity, authenticity, empathy, awareness, and a genuine desire to grow? What if – instead of valuing money, status, obedience, power, and control – our culture prioritised freedom, respect, compassion, community, and honesty?

Creating such a world is possible, but only if we break through the status quo to reach a new understanding of our purpose in life.

Societies are comprised of people, like a lake is made of raindrops. If you alter the colour of the rain, the lake will change accordingly. If you improve the childhood of an entire generation, all of society will benefit.

Humans evolve, and so does our culture, and this process will continue ad infinitum, whether or not we are aware of it. With awareness, comes the ability to intentionally shift that evolution in a direction more conducive to long-term happiness. This is true for all humans. As parents, we have the biggest responsibility of all; the way we treat our children today determines the legacy they hand down tomorrow.

What if every individual were encouraged to flourish in their own way, with a default setting of loving kindness? What if, instead of holding our children to a standard set by generations past, we could create a new standard?

We view our lives through the filters of our own pasts, but when we remove the lenses of society, judgement, and our own childhoods, we are free to see our children's true colours.

We are taught from birth to view certain aspects of parenting as being *normal*. Power-struggles, rebellion, tantrums, discipline, reward, punishment... the list goes on. The truth is, none of these behaviours are normal, or necessary. Power-struggles, tantrums, and so-called discipline issues, all stem from the same problem – an awareness that something isn't right within a given dynamic.

Just as society has updated its former views on slavery and the subjugation of women, so too, will our collective cultural consciousness reject, and replace, our damaging views on parenting. The commonly accepted practices of today, are tomorrow's horrifying past breaches of childrens' rights.

This book may read like parenting advice, but it's more than that. *Raising Rebels* is a revolutionary manifesto, speaking out on behalf of children worldwide, urging society to reframe outdated perspectives to forge a better future.

Peaceful Parenting and Radical Unschooling are not *techniques*, intended to be employed at the discretion of those *in control*. They are integrated lifestyles of freedom, respect, and love.

Dayna Martin's deeply personal exploration of

her own parenting experience has much to offer those trapped in the frustration of control-based parenting. Dayna's chapters, written over the course of many years, are presented non-chronologically, and delve into many of the most (traditionally) anxiety-inducing aspects of parenting. Food, sleep, hygiene, bullying, swearing, and independence are just a few of the topics Dayna tackles.

Dayna Martin has chosen to reject commonly accepted views on parenting. She lives the words she speaks. This book is *not* a collection of theoretical advice. It is liveable, achievable, beneficial wisdom, based on a lifetime of lived experience. Dayna does not make hollow promises, or tout empty words. She opens a door into her world, in order to share what she knows. It takes an incredible amount of bravery to expose yourself, in all your truth and vulnerability, *knowing* you will be misunderstood by most, and condemned by many.

So why has Dayna written this book? Why is she so open and honest about her life, despite the criticism it often brings her?

Because improving the world is more important than being accepted by it.

Some people, like Dayna Martin, live by example, follow their own path, and rest in the knowledge that the impact they have on the world will smooth the way for those who follow in their footsteps. It isn't always easy to swim against the current, but with enough momentum, we can turn the tide.

Our children are precious. They don't deserve to perpetuate a paradigm in which *success* means anything other than *to live with integrity, compassion, and love.*

Dayna's words resonate with me, and my family, on a deeply personal level. I am human, and I make mistakes, but I strive to provide a life of freedom and respect for my children, to the best of my ability. Whenever I read Dayna's words, I hear the truth in what she is saying, because I see it unfold every day, in the lives of my children.

It is within all of us to re-colour the world, and the most lasting changes live within the way we raise our children.

Remember – to *raise* is to *elevate*. Semantics? Maybe. But there is truth there, too.

Your children do not need to be controlled. It is not in their best interests to be mindlessly obedient. The worst crimes in history were committed by those whose default setting was *to obey.*

Conversely, the most revolutionary movements

and innovations throughout history were birthed by rebels, who dared to think differently.

We need to oppose, and therefore change, the way we view the purpose of parenting.

We need to reject the cultural norms of the society in which we live.

We need to *be* rebels, to *raise* rebels.

Nanci Nott

RAISING REBELS

CHAPTER 1

HOW TO BE GRATEFUL FOR YOUR CHILDREN'S MESSES

This morning I woke up to a mess on the floor. With four kids, this is fairly common. What isn't common, is my view of our daily messes.

Living this life with my children, and exploring their passions daily, involves a lot of facilitation, cleaning, assisting, supporting, and connecting.

I had an important realization many years ago; I realized that if I wanted to live a life of freedom and peace with my children, I had to begin seeing our home as something more than just a place to display our things.

I realized that our home is not just mine. It belongs to *everyone*. Therefore, my children's needs for our home are just as important as my needs for our home. Thus began my awakening into how to relax (and breath!) around the daily messes. I learned how to view them differently.

My need for a clean and organized home does not override my children's needs to use our home as a workshop of their interests.

Our kitchen is used as a science laboratory; a place to dye fabric, and make paper. It's a rollerblading rink, a place to bake with reckless abandon, a greenhouse, a think tank, and (occasionally) a place to practice yoga handstands.

Right now, our living room is a computer lab, a crafting center, a Bionicle village, a Call of Duty marathon space, a snack tasting center, a library, a study, and a wrestling arena.

Our bathroom is used – not only for washing – but for dyeing hair red, and pet grooming... among many other messy things.

When I see a mess, I see learning. I see memories being made. I see joy and growth.

What I feel, in turn, is gratitude – deep and powerful gratitude. When I wake up in the morning and see a mess, I think about what the kids made with the materials the night before, after I went to bed. What's left behind is a story of their creation.

Instead of getting pissed off, and huffing obscenities under my breath, I clean up their mess, and smile. I feel such love in my heart for having happy, healthy children, who are so creative, and passionate about life.

Instead of feeling resentment that they didn't clean it up themselves, I feel contentment, and acceptance that life (with four children who are Unschooled) is messy and busy.

This is such a short season in my life. I have compassion and understanding that, if it is late, and my children are creating, they don't always have the energy to clean up before bed.

My children know they have the freedom to leave their mess until morning – without fear of repercussion – because their needs matter, just as much as mine do.

There are (rare) days when I look at the mess, and I need to take a deep breath; releasing deeply ingrained conditioning of victimization and resentment.

Sometimes, I look at a space that I've just cleaned, and see a pile of interest-bits there again, and just can't get in that head-space of gratitude. However, those days are *very* few and far between. I know it's important to honor those days, and ask for help – which is almost always met with love and gratitude.

You see, when you don't clean up your home in an energy of resentment and frustration, you aren't modeling that housework is tedious and unpleasant.

Instead, you are modeling gratitude, love, and acceptance. You get to *choose* how you feel when you clean your home!

I feel this same energy from my children when they are cleaning. This is important to own, and take responsibility for. If your children are resisting cleaning, think about what you've modeled for them over the years.

My children always have the choice to clean up their own messes. I will always help them, if and when they need help, and they will never be forced or coerced into doing so. They do choose to help, most of the time, and I know this is because of my positive attitude towards cleaning, and the freedom with which they live.

I know there will come a time when I long to see these scraps of fabric and pieces of yarn on the floor again.

There will come a time when all that remains are my own needs – and a clean, organized home.

In the meantime, I will continue to find ways to honor the needs of everyone in our family. I will continue evolving in new ways, gaining new skills, and reaching a higher level of awareness, in order to honor everyone equally, and powerfully, in our shared home.

This is an ever-evolving process. I've seen the incredible role that I have in creating for my children. I can clean and organize in an energy of resentment, or in an energy of gratitude and love. Either way, I am modeling something that will stay with them for the rest of their lives.

I choose to model a higher consciousness of respecting everyone's needs, equally.

I choose to live in gratitude for raising healthy, creative children, who are always learning, exploring, and having adventures together.

I am modeling peace and respect in ways that most children today never get to experience.

Our home isn't just a place to just display our things. It is the heart-center of love and learning in my children's lives.

Today, I am so grateful to have this awareness.

CHAPTER 2

TRUST THE INTENSITY

When Tiff was two years old, she used to scream for everything. She worried about so much. She seemed to be unhappy often, and this was so hard, as her mother. She wouldn't let me brush her teeth or her hair, and finding clothes that didn't annoy her was challenging. Everything seemed to be such a struggle for my sweet daughter. For years, Tiff's needs outweighed everyone else's in the family.

I honestly could cry thinking about how difficult and painful it was to parent a child like Tiff in all of her intense sensitivity. Loud noises made her run and scream. Changes were extremely difficult for her, as was not knowing exactly what we were going to do every day. Being spontaneous was nearly impossible because it would throw Tiff into such a distressed state. I would make sure she knew what was happening everyday, from hour to hour. She was a child who needed to know exactly what to expect, and I learned how to give her that security.

Tiff also has a gift, although it can be really painful for her. She has the ability to read others like a book. If I am slightly annoyed with something, she knows it. She used to ask me repeatedly if I was mad at her. I used to hug her, and share with her that I wasn't upset with her. I was just having difficulty with someone else in my life. She has always been able to feel exactly what I was feeling, so strongly, that I found myself needing to explain things to her that my other children didn't even notice, or care about. She is an extremely empathetic human being, and being her mother has taught me more about myself than I ever knew was possible.

Family and friends used to tell me that I needed to have her evaluated, tested, put in therapy, and medicated. Parenting a highly sensitive child, your intuition often becomes clouded by fears. I wanted what was best for her, and to respect her in every way possible. I knew that if Tiff was put in the system it would forever change her. I knew she would be bombarded by others trying to control her, and force her to be someone different than who she was. Instead of taking advice from others, I took the path of my heart, and continued trusting my instincts, and her unique path.

I want to communicate to other parents with a highly sensitive child, that this is such a short season in your lives.

We have never punished Tiffany for the way she voiced her needs. She has never had a time-out, nor have we used any behavior modification techniques. She has always lived in partnership with us. Our role has been to love her for who she is. We have talked, explained, discussed and connected, helping her to feel safe and secure.

I look back on the first six or seven years of her life as being profound for me as a person; my daughter has taught me so much about myself. I have learned that children never need to be labeled, medicated, or made to change, in order to have a happy and functional life.

Tiff has always been powerfully unique, and she is someone who knows how to get what she wants in her life. The very qualities that made it hard to be present with her in those early years have shifted, and are now some of her greatest strengths, and most admirable qualities.

Today, I look back on those challenging years with such gratitude. Tiffany is one of the most beautiful, confident, patient, and focused people that I know. She used to hate being around crowds, and loud noises. Now, her favorite place in the world is New York City.

She used to need so much help with tasks that others found easy. Now, she helps me with daily tasks the other kids find difficult. She used to hoard food and toys, now she keeps her room spotless and simple. She used to hate itchy clothes and tags. Now, she wears fabrics even I find uncomfortable. She has overcome issues others told me she would never overcome without therapy and medication.

I was fed lies based on fear, yet, despite all the pressure, I never gave in. I loved and supported Tiff through it all, and today, she is a whole person; body, mind, and soul.

Now that she has grown older, she is able to control her emotions more easily, and let me know when she is starting to feel overwhelmed. I help her by giving her coping tools. She trusts me, and listens to my advice. She sees me as a leader, and her best friend in life.

Tiff has taken up modeling, and her inner beauty shines through in all that she does. She finds her own success in life. She's had her own pet-sitting business, and helps others find joy in any way she possibly can.

Last night, Tiffany took her first hip-hop class, taught by a beautiful, loving teacher, whom she trusts. As I watched my daughter dance among the other girls, I began to cry.

Memories of my sweet daughter flooded my mind. I remembered the worry, the fear, and the pain I felt for her, for so many years, as I helped Tiff navigate her world.

Tears streamed down my face. I couldn't take my eyes off of her, as she danced in her perfection, and inner light.

She danced with a confident smile, and her head held high, and my heart was at peace.

CHAPTER 3

THE LABYRINTH OF UNSCHOOLING

We have been Unschooling our children since birth. It has been an enlightening, healing, and amazing journey to get to where we are today. It has taken us many years to fully understand the philosophy of non-coercive, respectful, peaceful parenting.

Just when I think we have reached our destination in how we wish to parent, I learn we have a long way to go before total enlightenment, peace, and ease with how we live our unique life.

The other day, I wanted to take my children somewhere special for a walk. I am forever searching for new experiences and adventures for our family, so I had the perfect place for us to visit. We went to a labyrinth.

I had never walked a labyrinth before, and I was awestruck by how sacred a place it seemed to be. We walked up and over a grassy hill to see this amazing creation, where someone had carefully laid down hundreds of stones to create an incredible walking path. The stones had been there for a really long time, because moss had grown all around them. It was just breathtaking. I knew we were somewhere very special.

A labyrinth is similar to a maze, but there is only one way through it. When you get to the center, and walk back out again, you have reached your destination.

My children and I followed the stone-edged path, leading in a circle. I explained to them that I was going to contemplate, while walking around it, as a note at the entrance had suggested. I never told them any certain way they had to be while walking it themselves, but as I went on, they followed closely behind me, in total silence. I wonder now what they were contemplating. I tried to be totally present, so I could really feel whatever emotions or feelings came up during this walk.

I experienced such clarity of thought. I'd known, in theory, what a labyrinth was used for, but I did not understand, on a metaphysical level, until I actually walked one.

Just as I thought I was reaching the center of the labyrinth, it swept me around again, even further away from the center than I thought I was. It was not frustrating to me. I was pleasantly surprised every time I thought I was coming to the center, only to be swept around again. I enjoyed being together, on this journey with my children.

During our last loop around, I could see the center was near. I felt a warm wave flow through my body, as a realization bubbled to the surface of my thoughts. With fresh clarity, I understood our Unschooling journey in a whole new way.

Our journey has been much like this labyrinth! Just as I think I am coming to a greater understanding and getting to the destination (the place I strive to be) I am pleasantly swept further around, as I come to even an deeper level of understanding, of this incredible life with my children.

As we walked back around, in the other direction, I was left to contemplate my journey.

Every time I walk my own personal labyrinth, I learn to let go a little bit more. I understand my children's perspectives a bit more, or I heal from my past a bit more. Every time around, I feel closer to my destination.

But does this labyrinth ever end?

When it comes to unschooling, does one ever really get to the center; the destination of their own personal journey? Or is it more about that long, peaceful walk – the journey – and not the destination at all?

I may never know, but I find great comfort in trusting that, as I navigate toward my own center of understanding, it will be peaceful and joyous, because we will be walking hand-in-hand through our own unique unschooling labyrinth, together.

CHAPTER 4

SEE IT THROUGH

All of our children have gone through times in their in lives where their needs were outside the range of what our culture would see as normal for a parent to support.

For example, Ivy nursed until she was almost six years old.

Tiffany would not let us brush her hair, as her scalp was so sensitive when she was younger. We had to come up with creative solutions to work through the knots, and it took hours, sometimes when she was sleeping, for me to gently comb through them.

Tiff and Devin co-slept, until they were around eleven years old.

Orion always, with no exception, asks for a wet

towel with every meal. He hates sticky hands, and whenever we travel, I always make sure we have baby wipes handy for him. He also doesn't like to go into the bathroom that is on the far end of our house at night, when it dark, without someone in the kitchen with him.

We have never felt the need to *make* them move through the many phases, or needs, sooner than they were ready.

There are times that it has been a challenge, when it was hard to meet everyone's needs at once.

For the last few years, Ivy has had a long bedtime ritual that I was a key player in. She would brush her teeth, and then she wanted me to say goodnight to her stuffed friend, Frosty. She would then have me kiss a stuffed bear and a stuffed pig she loves. Then, we'd lay and I would tickle her back. When she was almost asleep, she'd get up and go to the bathroom again, then crawl in bed, next to Orion; we have two queen beds pushed together in our room and we co-sleep with Ivy and Orion. When she was in bed, she would say something, the exact same way every single night, "Night Mom, You're the best Mom in the whole-wide world. Love you, sweet dreams," which I would repeat back to her.

Then, she wanted Orion to say the same thing to

me. There were times I was so tired, I would literally fall asleep before the whole ritual was over, after which she'd wake me, so we could finish.

For the last two weeks, Ivy has been going to bed earlier than the rest of us. She decided that she wanted to wake up earlier because she loves the morning when it is quiet and relaxing here, before everyone wakes up. She goes to bed before me now, and she hasn't asked me to do the routine once. It is just over.... done! Just like that, she naturally outgrew the need, because she was ready.

It wasn't a struggle, or a bad habit that she needed to break. It was simply that her desire and need evolved and shifted. She confidently and independently decided what she wanted for herself and because she was always supported through her dependence, she was ready.

I am *so* happy when the kids grow through phases in their needs, but not for the reason most would think.

I look back on Ivy's childhood years, where the routine was so important to her. I look back on the years with four kids in our bed, never quite knowing when that would change.

Although sometimes it was difficult, I am so happy that we've always respected the kids, and honored what they needed, despite the challenges for us as parents. We didn't take the easy way out by refusing them what they needed from us to feel loved, safe, and secure.

Going to bed and *not* having to go through a long, repetitive routine is nice, I must admit, but the joy in my heart isn't because it is over. It is because *we did it* each and every time.

As Radical Unschooling parents, we see our children's needs *all the way through,* until they organically and naturally outgrow them. We don't guilt, complain, shame, or force them to move through phases quicker, to make our lives easier.

We know from living this partnership based paradigm for so long that when a child has a dependent need, it is only through embracing and meeting it that they become truly *independent,* when they naturally outgrow the need.

Our culture claims that if you don't force a child to suffer through *not* having certain needs met, that they will never do things on their own. It is said that they will never outgrow needs until they are forced, or refused, by the parents. This simply isn't true – it is quite the opposite, in fact.

An unmet need doesn't go away. It just warps into a new need, leaving a child struggling internally to search for ways to get their needs met. A child loses trust in the parent, and the damage to the parent/child relationship is profound.

Today, Tiff brushes her hair more than anyone in the house. She takes meticulous care of it, and, being a model, she sees it as her crowning glory.

Ivy isn't still nursing at age eleven. She is vegan, by choice, and inspires others to eat healthily, and compassionately.

Devin has a space above the workshop on our property, which was once my childbirth teaching studio. He moved into it, and it is now his apartment, at only seventeen years of age. He didn't co-sleep until he *went off to college,* as everyone told us when they attempted to get us to kick him out of our family bed as soon as possible. He's been to Peru for five weeks with friends, and stays in Virginia, for months at a time, with his girl-friend's family; confident and connected to us as parents.

None of the fears carried by others about supporting my kids through their needs came true. Not one...

When I go to bed tonight, I will enjoy the ease of just climbing in bed, and holding Orion's little hand as he falls asleep.

I will take a long, releasing breath of gratitude for the life we live together as a family.

I will always look back on the years of Ivy's bedtime routine with sweetness and love in my heart, so very grateful that we did what she needed, each and every night, even if I was exhausted.

Every single time a need has come to an end, the joy in my heart for meeting it, for however long it was present, leaves me feeling beyond grateful that I didn't put my needs before my children's needs.

I honor, and continue to meet, each and every need that my children have; without judgment, and without resentment.

I know the result of compassion and trust with embracing their needs, and I will never regret doing so. I will always be grateful that I didn't listen to those who warned me, shamed me, or attempted to fear me.

Peaceful Parenting is an investment. If you do the work now, you are nurturing their development and growth so they can be whole, confident and independent people when they are ready. It is letting them know that you will be there, through whatever they need, even if you don't know the reason they need it. It is a practice of unconditional love, kindness and pure acceptance of **who they are.**

. . .

The results of respecting what our children need are powerful and real.

Our children are strong, capable and compassionate people who are helping to shift the world towards the kindness and peace that will someday heal it.

Let go of the fear of others, and look into your child's eyes. Know that only good comes from you being present for them, through every age and stage of their lives, when they need you.

You can not create a negative trait in another by coming from a place of love and trust. You do so by rejection, fear, and the inability to be there for your kids, emotionally or physically.

Let go of the cultural fear surrounding kindness, love, and compassion when giving your children what they are telling you they need.

Step into this new awareness. Embrace everything your children are reaching out to you for, right now, today and always. It is an investment in their emotional future, and one that you will never regret.

CHAPTER 5

THE EVOLUTION OF CHILDREN'S RIGHTS

Children are the most discriminated-against people in our culture today.

When we were children, we were controlled and abused, even if we were not aware of it. The adults in our lives used control as a parenting tool, because that's how *they* were raised. Much of the damage society needs to heal from, is directly related to how we are parented when we are young.

There is a better way — a more peaceful and respectful way — to live with children. This approach is revolutionary and influential, but challenging. It involves re-evaluating our role as parents, and *un-brainwashing* our minds, which have been conditioned by the institution of school.

I have faith that our culture is ready. Let me help you step into this new awareness.

We were raised in an era where the parental role was focused on *obedience* and *control*. As children, we were trained to believe that life was about taking orders, which, in essence, only met the needs of the adults in our lives.

Children learn what they live. Being raised in an authoritarian paradigm, children learn that forcing others to meet their needs is what life is all about. Living this way creates a cycle of narcissism, *that our culture blames on a parent not being controlling enough!*

Most people who choose to homeschool their children purchase a curriculum, and do what schools do, at home. It is the same model and mindset of forced learning, control, and injustice.

When parents follow someone else's idea of what they think kids should know at a certain age, it distances them from their children. Distrust of the child's ability begins.

When parents evaluate, grade, and compare their children to others, it cripples learning, and damages the parent/child relationship — the very foundation necessary for authentic learning and growth.

When children are respected, and allowed true

freedom, most of them choose to live life without school, and all the trappings that go along with it.

For our children, this means living life without a forced curriculum, or traditional school work. We do not break life down into subjects; we do not grade, or make our kids do workbook pages, or busy work. We trust that our kids will learn what they need to on their life path, to be happy, and in turn, to be successful.

This level of trust in children is virtually unheard of in our culture. Most of us were never trusted as children. This has led to years of healing for many of us, to rekindle our trust in our inner voices, and our abilities in life.

I see – every day – that giving my children freedom (in every area of their lives) serves to keep their internal voice, self-love, and creativity, intact and strong. Trust is one of the greatest gifts you can give another human being.

I do not look at myself as my children's teacher. I am not standing in front of them, pouring knowledge into them, as the all-knowing authority. My job is to give them as much of the world as possible, for them to learn and grow.

I look at myself as a facilitator of my children's interests and desires in life. I do not have to know all the answers. I do, however, need to know how to find answers, through the resources the world offers.

Through the internet, television, books, video games, day trips, vacations, community resources, and apprenticeships, we offer our children more than traditional schooling could ever provide. Our kids are learning that answers aren't always black and white. They are learning about different theories and philosophies, and are developing their own beliefs.

In short, we are raising free-thinkers!

Another critical aspect of protecting my children's rights is honoring the fundamental human right to *freedom of mind*.

We do not pry into their minds to assess what they know. Children today do not have this basic human right. Their minds are prodded continuously. This treatment of children is incredibly invasive, and is not an accurate way to discover what another person truly knows.

I believe that what my children are learning is their business, and that it's not right (or necessary) to continually evaluate them, or their knowledge.

Education is *not* the primary focus of our lives. Instead, our focus is on family connection; pursuing our passions and interests together. Happiness and love guide our days. Our children *do* get a phenomenal education, as a side effect of living a rich, joyful life.

Our home is filled with interesting things to explore and learn from, like music, art, games, and crafts.

Our kitchen cabinets are full of ingredients for cooking, and for experiments.

Our home library overflows with mind-expanding reading material, informative magazines, intriguing games, and puzzles.

Instead of viewing our home as a museum of our stuff, we view it as a workshop for our passions, and a resource center for learning and personal growth.

Children are human beings, who live in the moment, quite naturally.

Our cultural view is that they should always be preparing for the future, instead of *being present* in what they are learning and experiencing. Then as adults, we take classes, and read self-help books, in an attempt to get back to that natural state of *being present*.

Continually preparing kids for the future, is like adults having to sit in a classroom, against their will, all day, every day, waiting for retirement. How fulfilling would our lives be, if this was forced upon us?

Education is an integral part of life, but not before laying the solid, necessary foundations of trust, connection, and the joy of living together, by doing things we love, as a family.

We choose to put our family before the institution of school.

I cannot imagine needing to ask permission for time with my children, or having to live our lives on a school's agenda. That is not real freedom! The school's needs *always* come before family needs. To me, this is madness, and I choose not to have that be a part of our lives, at all.

We live our lives together, because we *want* to be together, as a family. Our kids *want* to be around us, and we *want* to be around our kids.

When you don't indoctrinate your children in school, the bond and connection you have stays intact and strong.

The idea of quitting something doesn't exist in our lives.

A child will complete as much as they want of a topic, until they are personally satisfied. When they've gained enough knowledge or information to meet their own needs, they move on.

Our children's work doesn't have to be completed according to someone else's standards. Unschooled kids can go as far as they choose in understanding a topic.

This aspect of natural learning is different than in a forced learning situation, where children are not only forced to finish things to someone else's standards, but are also graded on how well they perform.

The focus when it comes to learning is not on content, but on compliance and obedience, above all else.

We respect our children in what they want to know. Our children have ownership of their lives, and live with full autonomy. Our lives are focused on trust, freedom, and the belief that humans learn best when they are *internally motivated*. When their desires drive them, children will learn what they need to, and it will not be according to someone else's idea of what is best for them.

Learning is pleasurable when it isn't forced. Children *want* to learn, and figure out our world!

They do not need to be coerced into doing so. In fact, children learn *less* when we give them the message that we know best, and that they are not capable.

We are not all meant to know the same things in life. Children in school are all being forced to learn the same subjects and content. This is so unrealistic and unnatural.

Every human being has different strengths and skills. Through living true freedom with our children, we recognize this fact. Children living with their human rights respected have just as much knowledge as children in school, but their knowledge is perfectly catered to who they are as individuals. When a parent is actively facilitating learning, this is the most comprehensive and perfectly individualized education one could ever receive.

My children learned to read by being surrounded by the written word. It is *total immersion learning.* When our children ask us how to spell something, we do not quiz or test them; we share the answer, and act as a valued resource. We don't ask condescending questions to quiz them. We don't tell them to go and look it up. *Total immersion learning* is honoring our children as unique learners.

My son, Devin, learned to read by playing online games. He was so motivated to play the game, and chat with his friends, that he picked it up very quickly. He learned when his mind was ready, and when he was internally motivated, because reading was a tool in his life to help him get more of what he wanted.

Reading, writing, and math are tools to help us get more of what we want (and need) in life. These useful tools would be learned quickly, if we weren't so convinced that learning them was tedious and difficult, taking years of practice, training and focus.

In our lives, these tools have been picked up easily, quickly and naturally. I think schools want to lead us to believe that learning the basics is something that they own the patent to. Don't buy into this lie, just because of your own experience in school. It wasn't learning to read that was difficult. It was the timing and method that created the illusion that learning was painful.

Our children's interests and passions are something we respect as an extension of who they are. I do not judge one interest as having more value than another. I see the learning in all that my children do, and not just what schools deem as worthy to learn.

We were brainwashed to believe that only school subjects hold value. It takes time to undo this deeply held belief, but it is essential to embrace natural learning. I believe that the most important *subject* in my child's life is *whatever they are interested in*.

My children's interests are the nucleus of their learning at any given moment. Although we don't break life down into subjects, if you were to dissect my children's interests, you would see that they touch on all of the traditional school subjects, and more.

We live life with passion, and facilitate their learning in the same way. In doing so, our children get an education perfectly catered to who they are as individuals, without ever having to force them to do anything they don't want to do.

We live in a world where parents are told to control and modify their children's behavior. They are told that this is the goal of parenting. Most parents take pride in how obedient their children are, and feel embarrassed when their children do not listen to them.

Not very long ago, men were told to beat their wives if they didn't obey. Men were encouraged by their fathers, friends, and leaders to punish their wives harshly for disobedience. Look how far we have come since then! Men would be arrested, if they lived this way now.

I believe that the same evolution is happening with children and their rights. We are on the cusp of change. In time, we will look back on these days with disgust and regret. When we can acknowledge the injustice (that children live through being controlled, punished, and forced to live a subservient life), we can begin to heal ourselves from our own upbringing.

I have never punished my children. Yet, they are compassionate, caring and respectful people. I have always focused on the needs under their behavior, instead of attempting to control them. I open my heart to understanding that children are doing the best they can, with what they know, at any given time.

I know many adults who can't control their behavior after thirty or forty years of life experience, and yet, we expect children to be able to control their emotions after just a few short years on Earth. We have very unrealistic expectations of children in our culture.

Parents today do the best they can with what they know. Yet, many are feel empty, and wonder why their kids don't like them, or want to be around them.

We hear words like *rebellion,* and chalk it up to normalcy. But what if there was nothing to rebel against? What if we lived the same respect for our children we demand they have for us?

What if we could recognize that the *punishment model* is injustice, and that, through using power to control another person, we are teaching them to do the same?

Through kindness and understanding, our children learn to love, and learn peace. In turn, they will reflect this back to the world.

Families who live in peace and freedom do not usually deal with *rebellion* from their children, because we are never the wall standing between them and their desires. In fact, we see our role as helping our children get what they want in life. We move from power struggles and control, to connection and partnership.

When we make this shift, we discover the love, and the deep feelings of joy, that we are naturally meant to experience as parents.

Adults interact with children very differently than they interact with adults. They are constantly training them: *good job, bad job, don't do that, do this.*

This incessant control and judgment is an unnatural way of interacting with another human being, who you value and love. Children instinctively know this, and feel the negative energy of control from the adults around them. Living in a role as your child's trainer meets the needs of the government, who want this breaking-down-of-children, so they don't become free-thinking adults!

Authoritarian parenting does *not* meet our needs. It only meets the needs of those in power.

There is a huge distinction between authoritarian parenting, and partnership parenting. One way meets the needs of the parents *only*. The other, respects the needs of everyone in the family, equally.

People do not see training a child as being unkind, but it's very frustrating for the child to have someone attempting to control their behavior all the time, never valuing (or understanding) the true needs under their behavior.

Children are not adults. Being in a relationship where they are constantly being prepared for adulthood, never allows them to feel the true joy of childhood.

Respecting children's rights and freedoms is a revolutionary approach to parenting and education, and it is sure to change history.

This is a parenting philosophy on the leading-edge of new thought, yet it is rooted in instinctual wisdom. The partnership parenting paradigm is gaining momentum. Our culture needs to realize that living with respect and freedom is the most responsible way to create a peaceful world.

The way our government, institutions, and media are telling us to parent only perpetuates the authoritarian paradigm. This distances us from our children, and robs us of the joy we are all meant to have, by nature, as parents.

Take back your lives, and the lives of your children! Take the freedom and joy that is waiting for you! Begin to unlearn, and relearn, a better way!

Children learn what they live. If we live in partnership with them, they grow up living with this worldview, and bring respect, kindness, and peace to the world.

Freedom is waiting for you, and your children, in ways you may have never considered before.

Join the Evolution Revolution!

CHAPTER 6

TRUTH BE TOLD: RADICAL UNSCHOOLING VERSUS PERMISSIVE PARENTING

Over the years, Radical Unschooling has been mistaken for permissive parenting. Many judgments have been made about it, based on this misbelief.

The truth is, Radical Unschooling is an extension of Attachment Parenting. It is a very hands-on, involved approach, based on connection, rather than control.

This philosophy is about being a child's partner, and focusing on their true needs. It's about helping them get what they want in life through partnership and love, rather than using behavior modification to force a child into meeting the parent's need for compliance.

Radical Unschooling honors the child's needs

just as much as the parent's needs. A side effect of this, is that children grow up learning that everyone matters equally, not just those in power. After all, children learn what they live!

Most people don't know other options, aside from control. The only other thing they 'know', is that we are being hands-off, or permissive, if we are not punishing or controlling the behavior of our children. They view anything other than traditional parenting as neglectful, or lazy, because they have never learned another way.

The 'experts and authorities' in our culture have done a very good job at selling people *the need to be controlled*.

Those raised in an authoritarian paradigm were told it was all *necessary,* and *for our own good*, and that it was *done out of love*.

It was confusing to be trained to meet the needs of the adults around us. Our behavior was all that mattered. Having negative intent assumed from us chipped away at our self-esteem. Being told that power and force is necessary, and that without it, we are not loved or cared for, is one of our culture's biggest lies; one that has been spoon-fed to us for so many generations it has become a collective belief.

Our culture indirectly tells us that being nice,

and respecting children, is neglectful and lazy. People do not realize how brainwashed they must be to believe this message!

They also don't see that this lie has been passed down for so long, because of the mental anguish it would cause us all if we *didn't* buy into this idea.

People aren't ready to see that the disrespect and mistreatment wasn't necessary for *their own good.* People don't want to face the truth, because it won't allow them to go on controlling, punishing and training their children, any longer. It would force them to finally validate the inner knowing of injustice that was prevalent in their own upbringing. It would compel them to do something *different*, and, dare I say it, *better.*

Radical Unschooling is not easy, nor is is lazy. It takes time and effort to find ways to meet the needs of everyone in the family, and respect everyone equally!

It takes listening, problem solving, and critical thinking. It takes patience, understanding, and discussion.

Some people in our culture don't want things to evolve. They want to force others to meet their needs, rather than taking responsibility for meeting their own. They are *very* resistant to honoring the basic human rights of children. They desperately want to hold on to an authoritarian paradigm, because without it, they need to step up, and take full responsibility. Many will still choose the easy road (of forcing children to obey them) but not without dire consequences to their relationships, and the connection they have with their children.

Ignorance is comfortable and easy. Facing the truth causes great pain in our culture, but it is here, staring us all in the face. Children's rights are next on the human rights agenda.

So many of us are saying, "Radical Unschooling is *not neglectful* permissive parenting!"

It is *not* lazy, abusive, or hands-off.

This lie can not be passed down any longer, because an uprising is happening. Children and teens are seeing the option for kindness and respect themselves, through the eyes of others being raised with respect and human rights.

You can't repress a conscious, aware generation. The lie can't survive in a culture that isn't buying into it, anymore.

I hope this helps you see that there is a lot our culture has yet to learn.

Radical Unschoolers walk a path of loving and respecting our children as humans beings, not as property. We are raising the bar, on so many levels. Many people aren't ready for it, but awareness can't be stopped.

We are here to share the truth, and open the door to understanding a more respectful, peaceful way to treat children; a way that models (and creates) peace, love, and connection with the world.

Are you ready?

CHAPTER 7

PRACTICE WHAT YOU PEACEFULLY PREACH

We have been conditioned by society to obey our masters, and answer questions when asked. However, as free-thinking individuals practicing peaceful parenting, we should never do this. Unless we are inspired to connect and share, we owe no one an explanation for the choices in our lives. In this chapter, I offer you a perspective that you may have never considered before. Just because someone asks you a question about your life does *not* mean you are ever obligated to answer. In fact, doing so models subservience to your children. If you want to raise powerful, confident, and free-thinking human beings, you must model how to live in freedom and peace. You must *be* the change you hope to cultivate in your children.

When confronted with questions from others committed to finding fault with peaceful parenting, you can use the 'pass the bean dip' response, which was first described by Joanne Ketch.

J oanne writes:

The 'Bean Dip Response' is best used when you do not wish to defend or engage with a person over a parenting choice. If you are discussing issues with a person and you welcome their feedback, the Bean Dip Response is not needed. I have found that new moms often confuse boundaries and when trying to convince someone of the rightness of their choices. It is best to assert your boundary and not try to defend your choice. Parenting choices should be on a 'need to know' basis. Most people don't 'need to know'. If asked, "How is the baby sleeping?" Answer: "Great! Thanks for asking! Want some bean dip?"

Be joyfully vague when it comes to others asking about something you aren't comfortable sharing. Unless someone is truly interested, avoid questions, and maintain a positive attitude. If possible, shift the focus of the conversation to something you may have in common, rather than stepping into a power struggle.

Most importantly, remember that when someone asks you a question, you should never feel as though you are obligated to answer. You can be kind in how you go about this. If you want your children to learn peaceful communication, you must learn and practice this yourself. Children learn what they live, and it is through your modeling that they learn how to own their power, their freedom, and their rights as human beings.

Our children's lives are sacred. Someone needs to authentically earn the right to hear details their lives and our reasons for parenting the way that we do. It is not something that I offer up to just anyone. Part of shifting to a partnership-based paradigm means that we need to begin taking back our the power that was given away to others for much of our lives through conditioning that many of us received growing up in the authoritarian paradigm.

It is not impolite to decline to answer someone

who is asking from a place of negative intention or judgment.

Take back your power as parents and be your children's voice when they are unable to be. Smile, and kindly share how wonderfully your family is doing, and offer to send a few links to better understand peaceful parenting and Unschooling, if they truly want to learn about it. Other than that, focus on what you have in common with people when engaging in a discussion, and guide the conversation to speak about what you are comfortable sharing about.

Articulating peaceful parenting philosophy can be challenging, and if you are not comfortable in communicating about this, you never have to. It isn't rude or unkind to choose not to explain your choices to those who aren't invested in your families welfare.

Answers to questions about your life with your children are sacred and personal. You don't owe anyone anything other than what that which you wish to share. You never have to defend your choices to anyone. In fact, doing so is stepping into an energetic power struggle is usually and can be a negative experience. Defending your decisions is rarely necessary. Due to cultural conditioning, we unknowingly give away our power in subtle ways without realizing we have a choice.

Byron Katie says, "Defense is the first act of war," and I truly believe in what she is trying to convey. The mere act of defending your choices is choosing to engage. Think about that the next time you feel the need to defend your choices.

As a child advocate, and a voice for peaceful parenting and Unschooling, if I invite you to ask me questions I am happy to answer you authentically, with passion and love. However, this does not mean that I do this for everyone.

Confidence in peaceful parenting is essential to fully embody the philosophy as a whole. It takes time to get there. It can shake the foundation of your inner knowing to feel pressure to articulate the details of your life philosophy to anyone who asks.

I know from experience that speaking about parenting choices, one needs to feel safe and accepted to do so with the greatest impact. If you aren't feeling comfortable, it greatly affects how you respond, and when you don't share from your heart, in a confident sincere way, it can undermine your message, leaving you to feel insecure and ineffective. In essence, you will spend your time defending your choices.

If someone asks me about my family life, I am often vague in my response, if I feel that the person asking isn't invested in learning from me, or if I sense that their intention is negative. If I am sharing with you, it is because you've earned trust or respect from me as a person, or as a group or community. When I share my life, I share my heart, and that is a vulnerable place to speak from. When one feels unsure, unsafe or defensive, the energy conveyed when sharing about freedom and peace can feel conflicted and negative to those challenging your choices. This is why feeling accepted, safe and comfortable is important when speaking from my heart.

If my heart is closed, my energy is in conflict with my words. If I am fearful, I can not accurately describe *trust*. If I feel defensive, I can not fully explain *peace*. If I am feeling judged, I can not fully share about *connection*. If I feel fear, I can not embody *love*. It is only through feeling, trust, peace, connection, and love that I can share with authenticity and passion.

I invite you to cultivate values surrounding what you find acceptable when engaging with others about your choices. We need to heal collectively, and become aware of the lingering cultural conditioning many of us still have in the spaces of our hearts that we may not be unaware of.

A childhood of forced compliance, and submission to those demanding answers from us as a child, takes years to heal from. It doesn't happen at once. We must learn to observe our emotions and feel the energy we convey to others in each unique situation. As we become more confident we become more clear in our choices. When we aren't looking for others to approve of us, their opinions generally don't affect us.

Understand that you can not speak your truth if you feel fearful or insecure. It is important to do the inner work necessary to embody freedom, peace and love through being honest with yourself in each and every interaction with others.

If you want to fully convey what you are feeling in your heart, you need to feel peace, connection and acceptance with those you are sharing with.

Respect your children enough to not feel the need to defend their lives to people who are dedicated to finding fault in the way in which they are living. Honor yourself, and choose wisely in who you connect and share with. Learn to recognize the intentions of others, and save your explanations for those who value what you have to say.

Be a voice for what you believe in and model the freedom, self-love, and peace that you want for your children and for the world.

CHAPTER 8

SHOULD CHILDREN EAT
WHATEVER THEY WANT?

Freedom with food is one of the most challenging aspects of Radical Unschooling, for most parents striving to live a more peaceful life with their children.

Some have asked me, "What if you child wants to eat sugar all day?"

My response is always the same: Control causes an unnatural dynamic to occur between a child and food. A child will want what the parent is attempting to control in abnormal abundance, in an attempt for autonomy.

However, parents see this behavior, and assume it is children simply *making poor choices without control,* They think children would do nothing but eat junk all day. This simply is not true.

When a parent is controlling something, it warps the child's relationship with whatever is being controlled.

A human's innate desire for freedom and autonomy is strong, and when being controlled, a person will overdo, abuse, and do things that aren't natural or balanced, for them.

The need for autonomy, choice, and freedom are at the forefront, always. In short, even subtle control and coercion can cause imbalance.

When living in partnership with your children, and not controlling them, they are able to find true balance with what feels best for them and their bodies. This is coupled with trust. When you're living with trust for your children, and not fear, you usually do not feel the need to control.

My children believe me when I share information with them. They do not think that I am inadvertently attempting to control them with fear-based information.

We research together, watch documentaries, and they truly want their bodies to be healthy! Who doesn't? This is amazing to those who have never experienced this with children before.

I do think it is important to have balance as a parent yourself, and not live in fear.

I sometimes crave something, like chocolate, and do not feel guilty for indulging, with moderation. I know that my body is resilient and strong. More often than not, I support my children in their desire to give in to a craving, because honoring these moments of desire enables us to be balanced and healthy.

My children would never desire to "eat sugar all day long," anymore than I would. I have total freedom with food, as do they. We lead a healthy life, where they desire to learn about how to keep their bodies healthy.

Devin and Tiff have both done their own research, and have the freedom to form their own beliefs surrounding nutrition and wellness.

My children have the freedom to eat what they want. Currently, Devin is Paleo. Tiff is vegan, and Ivy eats very healthily. Orion sticks to the few things he likes right now. I eat a high-raw diet. We all have the freedom to choose the diet that feels best to us. I shop, based on what the kids want, and prepare whatever they'd like.

Based on his own research, Devin prefers that I purchase free-range, organic meat. So I purchase it at a farm down the street. He has researched homesteading, and ideally wants to hunt for his food.

Tiff & Ivy, my daughters, are very much against his desires, so at this moment in life, they have many discussions/arguments about who is 'right'. They all have fabulous points about sustainability, animal rights, freedom and nutrition. I support them all!

I do not judge my children's choices. I respect them. I know that what they choose to eat is an extension of themselves. I know that if I say that what they are eating is *junk*, they internalize this. What does this do to their bodies when they eat what Mom judges as *junk*? What does consuming what you judge as *junk* do to you? Everything I put into my body I view as nourishing, no matter what it is. I believe that what you feel about the food you eat is just as important as what you are actually eating.

It is through true freedom and respect that my children have balance, and have discovered their own path to wellness. They respect what I say and use information that I share as a valuable truth to them. They look at me as a guided resource, and believe what I share with them. I am never standing between them and their desires. They know that I value and honor their choices in life. It is through partnership and true autonomy that children discover balance, health and wellness.

CHAPTER 9

WITHOUT FREEDOM, CHILDREN MAKE UNHEALTHY CHOICES

To Trust Children, You Must Trust Yourself
Children make good choices for them-selves when supported by a connected and loving parent, who doesn't use their child's freedom as a tool to control them. When children trust their parents, they believe them. When there is no power-struggle, children know there is no ulterior motive by a parent. True connection, and trust, are the foundations of the relationship.

When a parent punishes, threatens, limits, and controls their children, all issues center around fear as the backdrop. Children will make choices that aren't healthy or balanced in an attempt to grasp at some sense of freedom in their lives. This is a natural, instinctual drive to be free that will override all else which becomes the driving force within a child, coming before health, balance and wellness.

When we threaten freedom in children, they can never truly be whole people. When freedom is threatened, it warps the human condition.

A loving, connected parent who doesn't force, manipulate or punish a child has much more influence in a child's life than a parent in an authoritative/authoritarian role. Living without punishments, and threats of freedom being lost, children are safer, healthier and can find true balance in all that they do; be it food, sleep, technology, hygiene, their connection to nature and their relationships.

The biggest issues that parents deal with today are profoundly affected by how our culture tells them to parent. Parents cause the problems, but rarely see how or why.

Authoritarian parents usually deny this fact, claiming that fear and control are their biggest tools to ensure their child's safety and health. They feel that their children can't be trusted, but they have never tried a more respectful, peaceful way. They scream "neglect!" and "lazy!" to parents who are patient enough to not let fear control them. They were probably never trusted as children, themselves, so they have no idea what it feels like. They are sadly mistaken, and the warping of the human condition as a result of such tactics, take a lifetime to recover from – if ever.

So, to you parents brave enough to be called *neglectful* and *lazy* for not using fear, manipulation, control, or punishments as the central focus of your lives, and relationship with your children, know you aren't taking the easy path. It takes great strength to focus on the needs of your children, and not merely focus on controlling their behavior.

It takes great confidence to walk with trust and instinct as your guide. It takes incredible patience to find ways to parent with peace, honoring the needs of your children with respect. It takes powerful love to care more what your children think of you, than what the world thinks of you. Know that there is no way to do this without judgment from others.

You will be ridiculed. You will be accused. You will be misunderstood. You will be called a bad parent. Just know that I, for one, will always have you back. You are never alone on this journey. Hold your head high knowing that you are a pioneer, paving the way for future generations. Keep on shining your light for others. It will be accepted, in time.

CHAPTER 10

ARBITRARY RULES: ABSOLUTE RISK

G rowing up, most of us were told by the adults in our lives that punishing us was necessary to teach us about consequences. However, arbitrary rules (and punishments for the sake of *teaching us*) model unrealistic circumstances and inauthenticity. These behaviors damage the crucial parent/child relationship. When we do this, the positive influence we are meant to have in our children's lives is deeply affected, and oftentimes destroyed.

Ulterior motives (through arbitrary limits and rules) are not honest, or emotionally healthy, and our children know it.

It is completely unnecessary to create arbitrary limits and artificial consequences, or wield power over our children to teach them that there are consequences in the world. In fact, doing so will create confusion and frustration within them. They will be at a great disadvantage in life, through built-up resentment towards the adults who are supposed to love them, but who are, instead, being cruel and unjust, all for the sake of *teaching a lesson* that they would learn naturally, simply through living life by our side.

There are real-life limits and natural consequences all around us. Our children experience them with us, and through our experiences. It is unnecessary and damaging to create them artificially in the home, when time spent controlling children could be time connecting with them.

Through discussion and modeling, our children have the benefit of a rock solid foundation of love, support and trust with us as parents. This is severely lacking in the authoritarian paradigm of parenting, and puts children at a great disadvantage in life.

Loving parents never need to be mean to their children to *prepare them for the real world*. When living in partnership, children learn authentically, without cruelty and hypocrisy as the backdrop of their upbringing.

CHAPTER 11

DON'T KILL YOUR TV!

I was recently watching television with my son Devin, who is a Radical Unschooler. We were watching the program, *Anthony Bourdain: No Reservations*, as we often do together late at night when my other children are asleep. Devin and I share a love of travel, and while watching together, my heart began to pound excitedly, as Anthony Bourdain shared his travels through Egypt.

Learning about food, people, and culture ignites such a passion within me. Having this amazing visual window into the world is a tool unlike any other available in our human existence. Television is an amazing resource for an Unschooling family, and one I am very grateful for.

As Devin and I clicked through the channels, we

were introduced to Italian cooking, and survival skills in the wild. We listened to infectious Salsa music. We became inspired by stories of hope. I was in awe of the beauty of the Grand Canyon, Niagara Falls, and the Florida Everglades. We connected as we watched beautiful dancers, gymnasts, and mountain climbers.

Together, Devin and I were able to witness true human passion and triumph. We felt excitement, joy and love. We were inspired to travel, to do, to see, and to experience.

Television is a window into possibility and potential. It is an amazing tool in our lives, and one I can't imagine living without, as a Radical Unschooling family.

There is a lot of anger surrounding television in the naturally-minded community. Articles about *Killing Your TV* are everywhere, and they are so steeped in fear and misinformation. This same type of fear (surrounding media) was present before the invention of the television, with radio. Before that, comic books were the target.

Television has only been popular in homes since the nineteen fifties. It is such a new invention, historically. The way many people react to something *new* is with fear, in our culture.

When used as a tool for expansion, joy, and learning, television is as valid and enriching as any book or resource available.

When television isn't restricted, and parents and children live in a partnership paradigm through Unschooling (rather than the cultural authoritarian paradigm), kids aren't afraid to ask parents questions about topics introduced to them through television.

There has never been a time in which any of my children were interested in watching something I was not comfortable with them experiencing. Television is not a means of escape for our children, nor does it create a power struggle, in which they need to strive for autonomy.

When a power struggle is part of the experience, children will watch programs they are not ready for, all for the sake of wanting freedom of choice. This is never something my children need to do, because they are respected in how much television they want to watch. They have complete freedom in this regard, and because of this, they only watch what they are ready for.

They have no interest in shows that are sexually explicit, or shows that are ultra-violent. Also, we have Tivo, so they never need to watch commercials, which I know are a big issue with a lot of people.

However, there are times we do like to watch commercials, especially around Christmas time, when we can see what is available in our world. We have a fabulous time together, seeing the new toys on the market, and we discuss whether or not they truly do what the advertisers claim they do. This has been an amazing resource for our children to learn about advertising. Sometimes we purchase something we've see advertised on television, and have a great experience! Other times, we learn the item wasn't what the advertisers claimed.

Living a life of freedom and respect with my children, I can *be* a free-thinker. I can see the benefits of things most people fear. I can bask in the knowing that my children are the proof, and that no expert can scare me into following their beliefs. I can truly trust myself, and my children.

It can be hard to let go of the fears surrounding media when first learning about Unschooling. Walking this path with your children requires an undoing of cultural (and even *sub*-cultural) ideals. Once you begin to value your own experiences (and your children's choices) over the fear and judgment of others, you are one step closer to living a free-thinking life.

CHAPTER 12

UNWASTED FOOD

I recently received a question about Radical Unschooling that I wanted to share.
Question:

"My daughter will constantly ask for food, but not finish it, or will ask for something, take a bite or two and then say she wants something else."

This was my response:

The overall reason I wouldn't make a big issue out of this, is because I choose *connection* over a *power struggle.*

I choose to make our relationship the first priority over worrying about wasted food.

The cultural idea of wasted food is a very conditioned way to look at a situation like the one you shared. Our parents, and their parents, lived with a very different mindset about these things. It was very much *parent-led eating* back in their day. There were many reasons for this back then, but times were harder, money and food were scarcer, and the authoritarian paradigm was prevalent.

Today, I choose to meet my children where they are, and get creative with the food they do not eat.

I've used foods they haven't eaten in soups, or salads, for the next meal, if I don't feel like eating their leftovers that day. I have placed what they didn't eat in the fridge, or given it to our pets. We also compost. There are many ways in which we can recycle food.

Unschooling is a time of rethinking, so much! You can choose to rethink your beliefs surrounding food, meals, and waste as well.

For dinner, Tiff always takes more food than the other kids. She never eats it all, but she loves the look and feel of abundance on her plate. She arranges it beautifully, and enjoys the process of creation on her plate. I don't try to change her, but support her in her needs. She enjoys feeling that she has more than enough. It is a very secure feeling to her.

There are times when one of us will kindly ask her to leave enough of this-or-that for everyone else, which she does. Also, I will just wait, and let everyone else take what they want, because I know I can just eat the potatoes on her plate, when she is finished.

I also think it is great that my kids *do* leave food on their plates, and only eat to fullness! Isn't this something we strive to do as adults, and oftentimes fail, because we were so conditioned as children to clean our plates to meet the needs of the adults around us?

When my children tap into their true needs and instincts, food is often left over. I really appreciate this as a sign they are being true to their body's needs.

Our children are aware that, as a culture, we are *very* fortunate in regards to food. We discuss poverty and starvation in the world, and their gratitude for their life is apparent. They are very aware and compassionate children. I do not try to make my children feel bad for their abundance, nor do I guilt them into finishing what is on their plates to meet my needs, which may be associated with my own cultural conditioning. I am always rethinking deeply held beliefs in order to connect more with my children.

Children often have a unique way of experiencing foods, and eating. I embrace this about who my children are. I am the one who can choose to connect with them and find ways to get creative. I could choose to force and coerce them into eating, but this would cause negativity and power struggles over mealtimes and snacks, which would damage our relationship, and create lifelong issues with food for my children. Instead, I choose to observe their choices without judgement, help them get what they want, and respect how they choose to interact with their food.

In my opinion no food is never wasted. If the money is already spent, what difference does it make whether or not your child eats it, or whether the raccoons and rats at the dump do? Seriously! I love the fact that we are feeding the wildlife and insects with whatever we do not eat.

I never see anything my kids don't finish as *waste*. I feel connected to every living thing, and know we are feeding an extension of ourselves in whatever creature consumes what we don't eat.

You'll never hear me tell my Unschooled kids to "clean their plates," or that there are, "starving kids in China," like many of us were told as children.

I will always honor how much they choose to consume, and then be joyful in giving our food back to the Earth in a respectful, loving way.

The idea of waste does not need to exist if you can see that we are all one on this planet. My children know this, and I am grateful they remind me of it, every day.

CHAPTER 13

LOVE IT FORWARD: EXTENDING RADICAL UNSCHOOLING PHILOSOPHY

As I prepare for traveling to Texas, and then Australia, for speaking gigs this fall, I am remembering a flight my family took back from England, where I was the keynote speaker at the first ever Unschooling conference in London.

On the flight home, there was a mother traveling alone with two kids, who were sitting next to us. Being such a big family, we took up almost a whole row of seats on the plane. As we took off, I could see the mother getting impatient with her kids. She had a two year old, and a child around six. The two year old was standing on the seat looking at the people behind us. The mother was so frustrated, and I saw her squeezing her daughters leg, really hard. She talked in a really low, angry voice, scolding her. My heart hurt seeing this.

As I judged this mother, I began feeling bad focusing such negativity toward her. I had a moment of realization that I could extend the Unschooling philosophy of respect and kindness to her, and see what happens. I could choose to focus on this mothers needs under her behavior, and see how I could help her, and her kids. I could maybe make a difference, and be guided by love and respect, instead of judgement and feeling superior. This was a pivotal moment in my life as a Radical Unschooling parent and advocate.

I quietly asked Devin if he would switch seats with me, so I could sit next to this mother. As we rearranged, I saw her look up at me with hopeless, tired eyes. I smiled at her, and tried to focus loving, kind energy toward her. I looked into her eyes, and asked her, "Are you alright? Can I help you at all?"

She slowly lowered her head, and started crying into her hands. She told me that she had been traveling for over two days. She was visiting her family in Africa, and she was finally on her way home to see her husband, who she hadn't seen in three months. Her luggage had been lost, and she'd missed her last flight. She shared that she was exhausted and hungry, and had absolutely nothing left to give to her kids. She said to me, "I'm normally much kinder to my children."

My heart opened to her. I offered her a hug, and when I did, she began sobbing. I told her not to worry, and that we would help her out in the last leg of her journey.

We rearranged seats again, so that Tiff was sitting next to her daughter, who was around the same age. For the rest of the flight, they laughed and played games, and watched movies together. This exhausted mother gratefully accepted our help. I walked her two year old daughter up and down the aisles of the plane. At one point, I looked over to see that the mother was sound asleep in her seat.

Our family happily entertained her children for over 5 hours. When the Mom woke up, I gave her a cup of tea and a sandwich. She looked refreshed and renewed. She hugged her daughters, and played with them for the rest of the flight, joyfully.

In the beginning of the flight, when I saw this mom, I judged her. I instantly built a wall between us. I viewed her and I as two very different people, with opposite parenting philosophies.

Devin and Tiff also saw this mother's actions in the beginning of the journey, and commented on how mean she appeared to be acting towards her kids. When I asked how I could help, my children also witnessed me shift from judgement, to understanding and love for this woman. It was a moment in my life of personal growth, and one that my children learned so much from witnessing.

When we judge someone, we don't know their story, or their path. We instantly shut down the possibility of spreading peace and love, and making a difference in the lives of others. When we can look beyond the surface, we may see ourselves in others. We have all been at our worst at times, and it hurts to have the eyes of judgement on us when we are needing support and connection.

For the rest of the flight, I chatted with this mother. Listening to her talk about her life and personal path was so interesting. We had *so* much in common. We laughed together over tea as our children played. I can't imagine how negative the flight would have been, if I hadn't shifted from judgement to love. I created a space for connection, and that felt so empowering!

As we were getting off the plane, the Mom turned and thanked me. She said I'd given her such a gift, and that she would never forget us. She gave me a hug, and in that moment, I knew I had grown as a person.

Since the experience with this mother, I have extended the core concepts of Radical Unschooling philosophy to others in my life. It is so much more than a parenting philosophy. It is a *life* philosophy.

Focusing on others' needs, rather than their behavior, is a tool of peace and connection that can change the world. I love that my own path brings me into ever-widening circles to extend the joy and respect further and further to others. This spiralling growth is never-ending.

The flight home from England was a turning point in my life, and the lives of my family. I can't wait to see who we can help on our next journey overseas. I am soon going to take a thirty hour trip to Australia, with Devin. I know it will be fabulous, because no matter who we encounter, if we allow love and understanding to guide us, only joy will follow.

 "If you judge people, you have no time to love them."

MOTHER TERESA

CHAPTER 14

WHAT REALLY SPOILS CHILDREN

When you give to your children abundantly, from a place of pure love, they learn generosity and kindness.

When you give to your children from a place of guilt or fear, children learn to buy love.

The difference between these two intentions in giving is one reason people believe that giving to children will spoil them.

When a parent doesn't know how to give love freely, they use things outside of themselves to replace loving, authentic connection. The results are the 'spoiling' of children when the intention isn't pure and from the heart.

Somehow, in the evolution of humanity, we lost our way. We were told that only bad will come as the result of giving our children an abundant life. Those who were used as the example of this idea seemed to have bad results because of giving to their children.

However, the examples were set for us by those who didn't give true, compassionate, connection-based, love to their children. Instead, they replaced presence with presents. They bought their kids things when they couldn't be there, through replacing themselves with material things in their child's desperate need for connection.

When a parent tries to buy their child's love, it is space and time apart from their child they are really buying. The child is confused by this dynamic, and begins to learn that love isn't an emotional feeling, it is a material experience.

The warping of the human condition, and the cycle of dysfunction, begins when a parent does this. The concept of giving to our children is observed and judged through this common, dysfunctional intention. Parents then become fearful of giving their children an abundant life, and children lose out on connection, presence, and the tools they desire for joy, expansion, and learning.

Giving in itself isn't what spoils children. It isn't through receiving toys, trips or new clothes that a child learns to expect such gifts, selfishly. It is the intention of the giving that creates healthy expansion (or dysfunction) within the child. One replaces real love; the other enhances it. One spoils (which means it hurts the child) whilst the other provides growth, tools, and experience.

Giving in presence, instead of in place of your presence, should be the goal when giving to your children. We live in an abundant world. Parents don't have to deliberately deprive their children in order to teach them that life is hard, and they can't always have everything they want. Children will learn this naturally through discussions about finances and by observing how we deal with money.

Many parents do not talk about money, bills or finances with their children. I feel they are missing a great opportunity for children to learn in a real-life context about how money works, how to save towards a common goal and how to give to others, generously.

Open up your financial life to your children when they show the interest in learning about it. They learn through your relationship with material things, money, spending, giving and saving. You never have to withhold giving, or intentionally deprive your children, for them to learn the lessons you wish to teach them.

It is through connection, love, and vulnerable discussions about money and materialism that children will learn the most. If children learn what they live, when you give generously to them and to others, they learn how to be generous.

When you withhold, to teach a lesson, they learn greed and fear.

Live with love, generosity and kindness and the lessons will simply be a side effect of how you live your life. The lessons we wish to pass down to our children are simple when we take responsibility for living authentically and honestly in our intentions.

CHAPTER 15

UNSCHOOLERS HAVE BEDTIMES?

L ast night, around ten, Orion told me he was ready to go to bed. He is only three years old. About an hour later, Ivy came crawling up the stairs, and said, "I love going to bed!" She brushed her teeth, snuggled in next to us, and asked me to tickle her back.

All of my children love bedtime. I know it is because they were never forced, or coerced, to go to bed before they were tired and ready.

Living the Radical Unschooling life, we choose to respect our children's natural sleep cycle. I believe this is the healthiest way for children to live, without a parent-imposed bedtime.

When others hear Unschoolers have no bedtime, it isn't exactly true. Unschoolers *do* have bedtimes, but only when *they* say they are ready to sleep. It is a very organic, easy, joyful process for my children, and something they have never had any issues with.

I know most sleep issues in children today are because of parents imposing *their* needs on the needs of their children. Unschooling allows children the freedom to choose their own bedtime, and releases them from the cultural notion that bedtime is a difficult process for parents and children.

With Radical Unschooling there are no power struggles.

Our children have developed very healthy, balanced, natural attitudes about bedtime and sleep.

Living a life in partnership with our children, we are changing the way parents have historically viewed bedtimes, and we are bringing peace and connection into the process.

My children *love* going to bed, just as I do, and we have the Radical Unschooling philosophy to thank for that!

CHAPTER 16

UNSCHOOLING TO END MATH PHOBIA

People ask me, all the time, how my children learn math without any kind of formal schoolwork. I share that they learn what they need to learn as they go through life, when it is useful to them. Math is a tool to help us get what we want and it is easy to learn when a person learns what they need to, as they need it, instead of being forced to practice with problems that are totally out of context for them, just to get the work done, most of the time, so that they don't get in trouble for not doing it.

Last night, Devin was trying to figure out how much yarn he needed to weave a few tunics to sell in his Etsy store. He figured it out, and placed his order with an online store. He shared this paper he used with me and explained his process, which I found fascinating!

Unschoolers do, indeed, learn math. Yet they never have to do tedious and boring workbook pages, or be quizzed to do so. Nor do they need to study something to memorize it for the test, turning math from a useful tool, to an abstract boggle of numbers that they need to fake or struggle their way through, out of fear that if they don't, certain freedoms will be taken away from them.

When a child's autonomy isn't at stake through Unschooling, learning becomes very different than a child who is forced to focus on what will be taken away from them if they don't jump through the hoops placed in front of them.

When you let go of all of that you think is necessary for children to learn math, you allow them to see math as a tool that comes quite naturally to them when they aren't forced, in a way that is out of context with no real meaning to them.

When there is no fear, no doubt, and no focus on performance, children can see math for what it is meant to be.

When math is approached like it currently is in our culture, self-doubt sets in. You learn you are either a *math whiz*, or you *suck at math*. This false illusion is usually carried around with people their whole lives.

Math phobia is prominent in our culture, and it is time that we ask ourselves why.

It is my hope that forced learning will be a distant memory someday, and children will be allowed the freedom to use math as a tool to help them reach their goals in life, instead of becoming a handicap and means of anxiety and fear, carried with them throughout their lives.

Times are changing, and Unschooled children are showing the world that they are truly capable to learn what they need to learn, on their own life path.

CHAPTER 17

CAN PEACEFUL PARENTING END THE MEAN GIRLS EPIDEMIC?

Tiffany, her friend Zoe, and I, recently went to the UK to visit my mother in England. I had a speaking engagement in Scotland, so it was a great time to go on a trip and explore Europe. It was a marvelous adventure. We have never brought a friend with us before to see my mom, so to bring Tiff's friend, was so much fun because we got to play tourist and show her around the many places we've seen visiting her there, over the last 20 years. England feels like a second home to me now, and returning feels so beautiful with the connections and friendships that I've cultivated. Also, being in my Mom's garden is my paradise! It's the best place on Earth to do yoga.

. . .

While Tiffany and Zoe were with us in downtown Spalding, they were interested in meeting some new friends. Mainly boys. What teen girls wouldn't be, especially when half the boys walking around in this small British town looked like members of the band, One Direction.

My mother and I enjoyed going in and out of shops, having coffee, talking, and catching up. We kept an eye on the girls and repeatedly checked in with them through texts and passing smiles, as we walked to the town center where they were sitting, looking beautiful and happy, drawing quite a crowd of boys around them.

Near the end of the day, Tiffany found me in a shop and came running up to me excited, jumping up and down. "I met the most awesome boy! I gave him my phone, and he put in his Snapchat!" Instead of exchanging phone numbers, teens give one another their iPhones to add their contact info on whichever social media they have open for them to do so. Snapchat seems to be the most popular.

A few days went by and Tiffany joyfully connected with, and came to know more about, this new boy in her life. She discovered he was from Romania, and moved to England less than a year ago. He and his family are travelers. It's a robust culture in many ways, and we've been learning so much about Romania since they connected. It's a fascinating and beautiful culture. However, they deal with a great amount of prejudice, especially in England. Tiffany learned some Romanian and Cata learned more English, while they texted and video chatted.

My parents decided to take us to the mall one day. I struggled with the fact that we could be out sightseeing and be exploring places that would enrich their lives being in a different country. However, the girls wanted to visit the mall, so we went joyfully, and took off for a fun day of shopping together.

Cata and his friend Cosmin met the girls at the mall. I could tell my parents had trepidation. I convinced my Mum that all would be fine, and that we'd stay in touch, and meet at a specific time. Plus, my Mom and I would have some much-needed one-on-one time, which, incidentally, was very special and lovely.

I bought new nightgowns and sexy, relaxing clothing to recover from my upcoming surgery. I was glad for our time, but in the back of my mind, I worried about where the girls were, as we hadn't heard from them in a while. We began shifting gears to try to connect with them physically, to figure out a time to head back to Spalding.

Both Tiffany and Zoe are Unschooled, and parented peacefully. They have never been punished, or parented in the authoritarian paradigm. They have never been in a physical fight, and although they both have sisters they have fought with, they've never experienced violence on the level most of us dealt with growing up. Even with Zoe living in New York City, she had never dealt with what they were about to, in the small town of Peterborough, England, so far from home.

Little did we know, as we shopped for nighties and socks, that Tiffany and Zoe were dealing with something neither of them have ever dealt with before. Our two American girls, and the two Romanian boys, were sitting on a bench in the mall. There were a group of British girls staring at them from a few feet away. Tiffany glanced over occasionally, noticing the gang, but continued with focusing on her new love, and the bliss and affection that the two were engaged in together. Zoe and Cosmin had become friends over the few days prior, so they were laughing, connecting, and enjoying one another's company.

Suddenly, one of the girls, apparently the leader of this group, approached Tiffany and stood right in front of her face – nose to nose. She said, "You look like a slut."

Now, keep in mind that Tiff and Zoe have never been conditioned to please others. They have never dealt with the self-doubt, common insecurities and fears many girls in our culture carry with them, and that most of us grew up with.

Tiffany looked at her, without flinching, and said, "Thanks! That's exactly the look that I was going for!"

She was joking, of course, but her response took the girl completely off guard. Tiffany turned back to Cata and smiled. She ignored the girl who was trying to start a fight, with continued comments that Tiff said, "Made no sense."

Again, the girl got in her face, and this time, tried something she thought would be even meaner. "Your eyebrows look like shit!"

Tiffany is an aspiring model and makeup artist, so she knew the girl was just trash-talking. Tiff said to her, "No. They don't. They are totally on-point."

The girl continued trying to set Tiffany off, but Cata and Cosmin finally stood between them.

"Please leave," Cosmin said, to the girls.

The lead bully pushed Cata with her shoulder, knocking him back, but Cata stood his ground. "Leave the girls alone and go away!" he said to them.

Tiffany told me this story, and it is as accurate as I could convey according to her words, but what she said next brought tears to my eyes. She told me that she said to herself, **"What would my Mom do in this situation?"**

She said that she knew that I would walk away. The girls relentlessly continued to try to instigate a fight with Tiff and Zoe, making comments about their clothing being ugly, and them looking *slutty*.

I was shaking, intently listening to the girls share about it all. I was so upset that these girls had tried to hurt them. My protective mother-bear instincts were highly triggered. However, I relaxed when I realized that something was very different about this altercation, in new and compelling ways, that proved the power of peaceful, partnership-based parenting.

Tiff and Zoe weren't even phased by the put-downs or meanness thrust at them by this intimidating gang of girls.

I shared this story during my presentation in Scotland, just after it happened, and it was one of the most potent examples of how living in a partnership-based paradigm results in children who are whole, confident and so very different than most children and teens today.

I can say, from experience, and from my heart, that parenting respectfully, rather than punitively, creates a unique invincibility in young people. They become quite impenetrable to the onslaught of insults from others.

I was in complete awe of how the girls experienced all of this. It brings me to higher levels of confidence and awareness that living this life creates strong, powerful, whole human beings.

Tiffany and her friends were finally able to get away from this interrogation and impending violence. They walked away, but a few minutes later, the girls found them again, and walked towards them.

"Hey sluts!" the leader said, to Tiff and Zoe. She tried to trip Tiffany, but Tiff stepped aside, just in time to avoid her foot, and just kept walking. The boys handled themselves with grace, and admitted later how desperately they wanted to hurt those girls back for their cruelty.

They shared that in their culture, that would never have ended up peacefully. However, Tiff and Zoe modelled something that they have never witnessed before. The boys followed their lead with peaceful and confident energy. They all stayed calm, and didn't let it shake the joy, connection, and memories they were all creating together as new-found lovers and friends.

The girls' peace spread, and inspired others. This in itself, is a profound statement for the power of self-love, inner peace, and being raised without authoritarian control. It keeps the spirits of young people whole, empathetic, and energetically strong.

When I was in school, and someone went toe to toe with me, it was fucking *on!*

If I was challenged, I didn't back down. I didn't feel as though I had a choice. I would fight, or risk being a future target. The reason for the fight didn't matter. The size of the person didn't matter. If I'd been in that same situation back at Tiff's age, there would have been blood, and it wouldn't only have been mine.

The inner beasts of pain inside teens that are controlled, living injustice, and dealing with abuse, are unleashed in such situations.

The angst that children carry for the disrespect, control, and assumption of harmful intent that they receive is unprecedented. The time has come to reexamine our past, and ask ourselves why we continue to treat children as subservient and abuse them in the name of discipline.

Everything we have ever believed in this regard is *wrong*.

In later examining (and speaking about) the mean put-downs, I've come to realize they would have deeply hurt me at Tiff's age, because I would have *believed* the girl's words about me. I would have doubted myself. I would have wondered if I was a slut. I would have stared at my eyebrows for hours in a mirror, thinking they did, in fact, look terrible and ugly. I would have thrown my clothing away, crying on my floor, wondering what I should do, or wear, or become, to finally not be treated meanly, and to live in peace.

That same experience, which my daughter handled so beautifully and easily, would have hurt my soul so deeply.

Being raised as a people-pleaser, as most of us were, in the authoritarian paradigm, you learn to emotionally split between who we are, and who to become, in order to stay safe. We lived multiple personalities for survival and it completely warped our humanness.

If I were Tiff, in that situation at her age, I would have been triggered and engaged in a fight, instantly, as my honor, reputation, and self-worth would have been on the edge of it all. The consequences of backing down would have been profoundly dangerous in me becoming a target for future bullies. The repercussions for me not fighting would have been a risk. Me fighting would have been a risk, also. I would have had freedoms removed. I may have never been allowed in the mall again. I may have been grounded, or suspended from school.

In the depths of the intense self-doubt, self-hatred, and insecurity that I carried as armor throughout my younger years, there would have never been a choice to fight or not fight. Both choices would have had risks.

I always chose to fight as a young person. I hurt many people in my younger years, in the name of protecting myself. I took karate for three years, and most people who started fights with me didn't know that I knew how to fight and immobilize them. I never started a fight, but I never lost one, either.

Tiffany and Zoe didn't deal with any of these issues. When telling the story, they shared that it was hilarious that strangers would want to fight, and be mean to people they didn't even know. Our girls did nothing to initiate this or give any reason why it could ever be justified. They were just pretty, confident young ladies, happy and alive. That alone is a real threat to others who are living as I did, in deep shame, insecurity, and self-hatred.

For hurting young people, taking confident girls down a peg is an illusion of control. In their minds, they somehow feel *better than* in doing so, which is profoundly troubling.

The angst inside those girls (from being controlled and mistreated at home and school) needed to be released somehow that day. Unfortunately, Tiff and Zoe wouldn't allow the mean girls' pain to be released upon them. Our girls were whole enough to not let it happen, and would not step into it that dysfunctional dynamic. It simply didn't make sense to them.

Tiffany and Zoe said that they knew the girls were hurt, and jealous of them. That in itself is the most liberating thing that I have ever heard a teen speak to me. It wasn't a snarky, egotistical way of communicating it, either. It was pure, mature and loving compassion for these girls who wanted to fight them.

Tiff said she knew she looked cute, and her outfit was pretty, and in style, and that her eyebrows looked perfect. She said she loved her shirt, and Zoe loved her outfit, also. They took time, effort, and pride in picking out the best look and makeup to have a fun day at a British mall, with these new and exciting Romanian boys that they met there.

As the girls walked away from Tiff and Zoe, one of the girls screamed out for Zoe to pull her shorts down lower, because they were so short that she looked, "like a slut."

Zoe never looked back, and instead, hiked them up as high as she could, to prove a point. You can criticize and challenge. You can put down and harass these Unschooled, free, peaceful and whole teens all that you want. However, they will not engage with anything but truth and integrity, as they know the truth about who they are. They always have the choice to participate, walk away, or speak with confidence.

We are freeing our children by living in peace and partnership. We are keeping them safe in many new ways, by being brave and forward-thinking enough to live this evolution in parenting. With every unique experience and every new challenge, my children show me that living this way promotes peace, love, compassion, and kindness.

To have someone step into your face, nose-to-nose, wanting to hurt you physically, and to be clear and balanced enough to realize that it wasn't about you and that it is about them, is beyond comprehension for a teen in this day and age. It is a great hope of mine for the future that more parents learn about how letting go of the punitive dynamic in parenting keeps their children and teens so much safer and more compassionate.

There is a new and exciting era beginning! It is pure and potent proof that love, kindness, freedom, and peace are the only way towards what we all want and peaceful parenting is an enormous part of this collective dream.

This experience empowered the girl's in incredible ways. They were excited to have lived the power and excitement of it all, which utterly floored me! That night, Tiff said to me, "Mom! It was just like in the movies! I couldn't believe it was all happening! Those girls were acting crazy, mean and jealous, but I know it was because they probably had bad lives, themselves. I bet they were abused at home. I knew it had nothing to do with us. I felt bad for them, even though they were all bitches to me."

For her to be bright enough to come from a place of holding such a focused, empathetic understanding of others pain was such an evolved perspective. It was an intense experience, for sure, but they handled themselves with confidence and utter grace, peacefully avoiding any physical or verbal altercation. Their heads were held high in pure self-love and understanding for the way that most teens today are forced to live. These *mean girls* wanted a fight. They wanted to release the pain and aggression they undoubtedly deal with in their own lives. when they should be receiving love and support.

These *mean girls* may someday change, as many of us have, to step into this reality about life, peace, love, and freedom. When others can see that it is such an unfair existence that most teens live today, they may be able to be treated like our children are, and more peace and change could come. Those *mean girls* wanted to ease their pain, by hurting the girls that day, but they were not able to do this with Tiffany and Zoe as their spirits are intact and they were impenetrable. They were full of truth, confidence and awareness and most of all; they were encircled with love, both physically and energetically, from us parents and those who show them their worth and beauty every day of their lives.

We learned a great deal that day, at that simple mall in Peterborough, England. The most important lesson of which was:

" The paradigm of authoritarian parenting continues to breed *mean girls*. Compassion can only be cultivated in children when parenting with a partnership-based model. *Mean girls* cannot fight other girls who are holding hands, instead of fists.

CHAPTER 18

FORCED MEMORIZATION IS ABUSE

The idea that anyone needs to memorize state capitals or times tables is outdated. Forced memorization is an obsolete practice of learning, in general. I suppose, it is a branch of learning, where many of us know things from being forced to memorize. However, I don't consider it necessary, or even healthy.

Deeply integrated learning is about the internal motivation and desire from the learner. It does not come through force by an authority.

The precious and sacred space, that is our children's minds, doesn't need to be taken up by pointless, mind-numbing 'information' that has no purpose or use to them in a real-life context. Instead, they should have the freedom to ignite the fire of passionate learning through living a life of their choosing, and doing what they enjoy with their time, through Unschooling. Learning will happen in real and powerful ways, despite your fears!

Freedom of mind is an often overlooked aspect of children's rights, because we think we know better than they do. However, a child's desire for freedom is a natural force within them, that drives their very being, each and every day. The more we deny them this freedom, through forced learning, the more it warps who they are and who they become.

The idea that our children should be filling their minds, like sand in a bottle, with all of the grains representing memorized information, is a flawed practice.

Instead, we can choose to smash that bottle, and expand their capacity to learn and grow, by respecting their autonomy and freedom of mind. The resources for learning are endless and can't be contained.

Our children will learn and grow in ways that we never knew were possible. We are the ones who should be open to learning from them, as they are much more graceful learners than we were ever allowed to be.

CHAPTER 19

RADICAL UNSCHOOLING AND SLEEP STRUGGLES

In our experience, our children's sleep seems to run on a seasonal, natural cycle. Our family changes our sleep patterns with the changing of the seasons, and we have always lived this way.

Much like cycles that follow the rhythm of the moon, when sleep is viewed from this natural perspective, one can see how it could be the most organic, intuitive way to live. In order for freedom and releasing control to flourish, one needs to step into a space of trusting children with their ability to tune into their natural rhythms. They can, without our interference.

Trusting your child to find balance, and naturally slip into a healthy rhythm for themselves, is an aspect of this life that is difficult for many. As important as sleep is, and as much as my kids have the freedom to sleep as much as they want, I have found that without outside stresses, and without imposed schedules and living other's agenda, their sleep quota is very different than what most children in our culture require. Their bodies run efficiently, because their minds and bodies are unhindered.

Sleep is time for our bodies to recoup from the day before. Children in our culture need that repair time for their bodies after a day of eating poorly, and living in a way so out of alignment with nature. Also, it can be quite exhausting living a life where one has to push up against control all day.

Sleep needs to be long and regular for children living in such a way. When you have a lot to heal, you need a lot of sleep.

This isn't to say that Radically Unschooled kids always sleep less. They sometimes sleep *more* than the average child, and this is good!

In our family, we all do this, much like how we eat. Some days we eat very lightly, according to the needs of our bodies. Some days our bodies are detoxing or needing different vitamins and minerals, and we crave and eat much more than usual. The same is true for sleep.

I am grateful that our children have the freedom

to tune into their individual needs in regards to sleep, each day, everyday. I believe that there is no healthier way to live.

Our kids have very *efficient* bodies. We provide great fuel for their bodies and they spend their days living without resistance.

They do not have to push up against the adults in their lives, to squeeze out even the tiniest sliver of freedom and joy. It is exhausting, unhealthy and damaging for a child to live in this way.

The way to ensure children get enough sleep to repair this avoidable damage is to give sleep requirements for children, which are backed up by doctors and experts, in the field of sleep and medicine. In our lives, we have no use for this information, as it isn't applicable to our lives.

Our children do not deal with the wear and tear on their bodies and minds that most in our culture live. They eat maybe 50% less than the average child, as we don't need nearly as much food as our culture pushes on consumers. Their bodies run efficient, potently and powerfully.

I believe that Radical Unschooling is truly how humans would live if there were no cultural or outside influences.

.   .   .

W hat our culture knows about children and sleep today, is wrong for *our* children.

I realize that it is hard to trust your child when we live in a culture that fears them, if they aren't controlled. Sleep is as easy and effortless as breathing. When you let go of the fear and the cultural conditioning, you will see how joyful and beautiful it is to step into the space of allowing your child to tune into their innate knowledge about what their bodies truly need.

CHAPTER 20

YOUR CHILDREN DON'T WANT IT

Y ou don't have to live perfectly, to be the perfect parent for your children.

When we can admit our mistakes, flaws, and issues, we are able to model one of the greatest aspects of being human – the ability to change. We have to *live* the reality of being human to it's fullest extent, for our children to see what life is truly about.

Most of our parents didn't show us much of their inner landscape.They were trained to believe it would be wrong to do so. Our parents, and most parents today, have such crushing pressure to be something they are not, in order to be good parents. They are told to become tough, consistent, and essentially withhold love, through control, punishments, shame and forced compliance, to teach children how to survive in the world.

That way of living with children only benefits those in power and have no doubt, it hurts parents as much as it does their children, to live in such an unnatural way together.

As parents on the brink of a new paradigm, we need to be brave enough to admit our mistakes.

We have to be vulnerable enough for our children to see us cry.

We need to be compassionate enough to change our minds when we see another perspective, and we need to be confident enough to become aware of and heal our deep inner wounds.

We need to let down the cultural armor that we've been forced to build up over the years to survive in a broken world. Slowly, with self-love and forgiveness, we can learn to take off our protective armor, piece by piece, knowing that we are finally safe and there is nothing for us to fear anymore.

Have no doubt – we are broken! De-conditioning takes years, and finding ourselves beneath it all takes great effort and inner work. It's a messy, and sometimes scary, experience, but there is no other way to become who we have always wanted to be, and who we would have been long ago, had we not been conditioned to be something else to survive.

Our children need to see how we pick up our broken pieces in our lives when we make mistakes – and we *will* make them!

We don't have to hide them anymore because someone will make fun of us, shame us or punish us.

Now is the time to let down all that we've been forced to build up since childhood, when we needed to protect our sensitive selves.

We need to become what our children need to navigate their world in a healthy, loving and peaceful way.

We need to walk through the fire of our souls, and look deeply at what we need to change within ourselves, and leave a trail of armor behind us.

We don't need it anymore and trust me, your children don't want it either.

CHAPTER 21

UPGRADE YOUR PARENTING VOCABULARY

I would like to share that being mindful of the language we use when describing our children's feelings can be a helpful step towards positive, peaceful, parenting. I would suggest moving away from the word *tantrum*. It is a culturally common word that dismisses the fact that the child is having true, real feelings. The term brushes off their true feelings making them seem bratty, suggesting their feelings aren't worthy or valid.

When children hear their feelings described as tantrums, it is embarrassing and confusing to them. It is also dehumanizing to judge another's feelings as unnecessary. This is exactly the energy you convey when using this word. I would never say, "My partner had such a tantrum!" or "My best friend had a tantrum when I told her I couldn't go to lunch."

Children deserve the same respect that adults do. There never needs to be a double standard.

Can you see how disrespectful the word *tantrum* truly is?

Remove it from your parenting vocabulary, and you will be one step closer to respect and connection with your children.

Snatching and *grabbing* are also terms that carry judgmental, disrespectful energy.

A child's motor skills are different than those of an adult. When they reach for something, which is normal and natural for a young child, it isn't as easy or as smooth-flowing as an adult reaching out to touch something. It looks faster, and not as deliberate of a movement. Looking through the cultural filter of an adult, we see disrespect, meanness, and selfishness. This is, in fact, not accurate to what is happening.

The words *grabbing* and *snatching* often imply negative intent and greed. How do you feel about the person who has this word described to explain their actions?

Children are naturally curious. Babies, toddlers, and young children aren't doing anything to be intentionally disrespectful to the other person. Children are often scolded, shamed and punished for *grabbing*, when in fact, they are so misunderstood!

It is excruciatingly frustrating for a child to be accused of doing something harmful or mean to another person, when all they were doing was reaching out in the only way that they physically can.

Children have the instinct to touch and explore something that is interesting and attractive to them. Their actions are quite innocent when seen through their eyes and heart.

When you make an effort to reevaluate the words that we use in regards to children, and focus on their well-intentioned and natural needs, we see that they are following how nature is guiding them.

Through shifting the words used, we shift the negative energy that has overlaid the real issues. Through this, we can move closer to Radical Unschooling and peaceful partnership-based parenting.

When a child has strong feelings, or reaches out to explore something in someone else's hand, rather than brushing them off, shaming them, or making it about you, begin to see their behavior with new eyes.

Release the notion that children are born *bad* and need to be *trained* to learn goodness.

Let go of the narcissistic, cultural perspective that whatever everyone is doing around us is somehow about us being a victim in some way.

Shift your focus from scolding, shaming and training to assisting, understanding and loving a young child who is expressing needs, and exploring the world around them.

Give yourself a **parenting language upgrade!**

Use words that carry a positive energy and message, and give your children the gift of being understood for who they truly are.

CHAPTER 22

LEARNING THROUGH TEACHING

My fourteen year old son, Devin, is a very creative person. He has recently started bladesmithing, which is making knives and swords.

Yesterday, he asked me to come outside and watch him make an entire knife from scratch. It was below zero out, but I bundled up and went out to watch the process. I watched him do everything, from getting the fire roaring hot in his forge with coal, heating up the metal, hammering out the knife, heat treating it, and sanding it down to a sharp blade.

I listened to his step-by-step instructions attentively as I opened my mind to learn something new. He was passionate about what he was sharing with me, and I could tell that teaching me was very exciting for him.

Teaching is an extension of true learning. Over the years, I have observed this desire to teach from my all of my children.

When Devin was only four years old he loved a television program titled, 'Avatar: The Last Airbender'. I can still remember he and I being outside together on a warm spring day while he taught me about the different powers of the various types of benders on the show. He gave me a stick to hold, and explained how I would defend myself to each of them. He was teaching me about what he knew, and I could see that it was helping him learn in the process of having me be his student.

Over the years, I have come across quotes that confirm the idea that teaching helps to solidify knowledge.

"What I hear, I forget;
What I see, I remember;
What I do, I understand."

OLD CHINESE PROVERB

Devin was very clear and focused when he was teaching me how to make a knife. He even had me try it myself, using the mallet to hit the hot metal. He encouraged and supported me through my fears of getting burned by the hot coal-fueled forge.

I was reassured by my son that I could do it, and I believed him. A certain level of trust for the teacher is necessary when one chooses to learn something new. With a forced learning dynamic, I do not believe that this trust is ever built, crippling the learner and teacher, placing them in a dysfunctional relationship. It not only hinders learning, but it creates an insecurity within the teacher himself, making him doubt his own knowledge and abilities. Forced learning of any kind not only damages the student, but it hurts the teacher, as well.

The act of being present through the entire process was a bonding experience for my son and I, further deepened the trust between us. He was my only focus, and I, his.

Not only did I learn the art and skill of blade-smithing, but I learned that my son is strong, powerful and capable in his communication.

When parents allow themselves to be vulnerable

around their children, something blooms in the relationship that few parents today get to experience.

When we stand as the student to our children, we allow ourselves to be seen in our incompleteness as humans. This vulnerability is essential for our children to truly understand that we are never done learning. Being a student is something that continues until we die. It is an essential aspect of becoming the people we are meant to be in life.

When our children want us to watch them when they are very young, we sometimes feel it is boring. We only give them a portion of the focus they are asking from us, because we already have obtained the knowledge they are trying to share with us.

"Mama, look!" is something many parents frustratedly (and half-heartedly) entertain for a fleeting moment.

However, this process of teaching another is critical on their path to mastery of an interest or topic. Being present, and being in the position of the student, helps your children by allowing the process of solidifying their knowledge. Do not overlook this important aspect of facilitating learning.

Allowing Devin to be my teacher helped him grow as a person. He not only gained confidence in his abilities, he was able to be a mentor, a teacher, and skilled supporter of someone else on their own path to learning. This give-and-take has been the pinnacle of partnership parenting over the years.

I am grateful for all that my children have taught me. I am still learning from them, and they from me. This dance will continue between us for the rest of our lives together. I will always proudly serve as their student on their learning journey!

CHAPTER 23

CHILD ADVOCACY IN PUBLIC

The other day, I took my daughters to a local shop that sells jewellery and accessories. There was a young family there, and the parents were talking in a threatening tone to their very young daughter. I walked closer to them to see if I could get a sense of what was going on.

They were attempting to coerce her into getting her ears pierced. The young girl cried, saying over and over again, "I don't want to! I don't want to!"

An older woman standing nearby was then coercing the parents into forcing their daughter to do it. She was giving parenting tips on how to take away the child's new toy and not give it back, unless she did as she was told.

My heart raced. I started sweating. I took a deep

breath, walked over, and said, "Excuse me. Would you be open to hearing an alternative opinion on this?"

The parents looked at me, and said, "Yes."

I shared with them that Ivy and Tiff decided to get their ears pierced at ages six and eight, and that it was a special rite of passage, that they chose. I shared about the girls' autonomy, and how the connection between them (the parents and the young girl) would be hurt if they didn't respect her choice. I also said that the trust that she has for them may be affected if they force her, against her will.

The father said, "Yes! I agree with that."

The Mom looked disappointed. I went on to say that I realized it was a personal decision, and that it was for them alone to decide. I shared that I wanted to offer my view, so they could make a truly informed decision.

They walked out of the store. They were still on the fence, but I was so glad I spoke up. It isn't an easy thing to do, especially when you have the opposing energy present, trying to convince them otherwise. My daughters were very proud of me tonight, and thanked me for, "helping that little girl."

Don't be afraid to speak up when you see injustice!

You can do it in a way that is peaceful, non-intrusive, and respectful.

Be brave. Be kind, and speak your truth.

The example you set for your children (and for others, when they witness peaceful communication) is desperately needed in our culture.

You can help shift the world towards more peace. The lives you touch will cause ripples that never end.

CHAPTER 24

DAMN UNSCHOOLERS!

My kids have the freedom to use whatever words they choose to use, every day. The truth is, my kids swear sometimes, and they are not punished or reprimanded for it. Yet, they are very loving, kind people, who just happen to have a freedom most children in our culture do not have.

When I feel the need, I admit, I swear too. I choose words our culture labels as *bad* or sinful, and use them as adjectives, nouns. and verbs every once in a while.

Words are only words in our family.

We do not choose to live by the old school mindset of, "Do as I say, not as I do."

I find the authoritarian paradigm disturbing, and disrespectful to children.

Instead, I know that if I choose to swear, my kids will swear, too.

I take full responsibility for this fact.

My kids have the freedom to swear, just as I do.

It's interesting to note that we *do* talk about swearing, and how it offends a lot of people.

Before new friends come over, Devin and Tiff ask me if it is okay to swear around them. Some families have kids who also have this freedom, and some do not. We share openly about it, and the kids always respect it.

Sometimes a swear will come out, and there will be a kind of "Ooops," look on my kid's face if they forget around certain people. It doesn't happen very often, though. I never correct them in front of people who don't like swearing, nor do I put any focus on it at all.

It seems so hypocritical to punish a child for swearing if you do it yourself.

Shouldn't we all have the freedom to choose the words we use? Isn't it a basic human right?

It is a double standard that adults are allowed to swear, and children are not.

I do see more and more parents relaxing around the issue of children and swearing. The list of *bad words* isn't quite as long as it was in my mother's day.

When researching before writing this, I came across this information, on Wikipedia, about swearing:

> *"Tape-recorded conversations find that roughly 80–90 spoken words each day — 0.5% to 0.7% of all words — are swear words, with usage varying from between 0% to 3.4%. In comparison, first-person plural pronouns (we, us, our) make up 1% of spoken words.[2]*
>
> *Research looking at swearing in 1986, 1997, and 2006 in America found that the same top-ten words of a set of over 70 different swear words were used. The most-used swear words were fuck, shit,*
>
> *hell, damn, goddamn, bitch, boner, and sucks. These eight made up roughly 80% of all profanities.[2] Two words, fuck and shit, accounted for one-third to one-half of them. [2] The phrase "Oh my God" accounts for 24% of American women's swearing.[3]"*

Children are historically punished for swearing. I know a few people who swear with every other word that comes out of their mouths. I feel it is as a result of being severely punished as a child for swearing.

When this happens, and a person *finally* has freedom of speech as an adult, they make up for all of that past control and swear *so much more* than a person normally would (which, on average, isn't very often).

My children do not swear any more than I do, actually. Sometimes Ivy will get stuck on a certain swear, and try it out for a while, and combine it with other swears in a creative way. *Assbitch* is one of her newest creative expressions.

However, our children *do* have a clear understanding of when it is okay for them to do so, and when it is inappropriate. They have respect for others who are uncomfortable with swearing, like family, and when out in public.

At a recent visit to my friend's house, she pulled out some organic alphabet cookies. The kids all sat together combining letter to make their names, and they also spelled out some swears. We laughed and joked with our kids as they explored some words our grandparents would have had soap put in their mouths for spelling out. It didn't feel wrong. It felt natural and light, and just another way to connect with our kids.

It is liberating to know that when it comes to children and swearing, we do not have to do what was done to the generations before us.

I think most parents today would be so much happier if they could just lighten up about the whole swearing issue. I think that if they gave their children the freedom to swear, they would realize children are receptive and respectful at times when it is inappropriate to do so. It would mean that, through less punishment and control of another human being, more joy and peace would naturally flow into the family.

Now.... ain't that *damn* beautiful?

 Nature knows no indecencies; man invents them.

MARK TWAIN

CHAPTER 25

RADICAL UNSCHOOLING READING: THE LONG HARD ROAD TO TRUSTING YOUR CHILDREN

All of my children learned how to read, in their own time, with support and facilitation. When my children ask me how to spell something, I spell it out for them. I don't tell them to look it up themselves. I am here, by their side, as a resource. I am up and down dozens of times each day, to assist my kids in whatever they are researching, playing, reading, or creating.

All my children came to reading as a tool to help them get more of what they want in life. Reading wasn't something my children feared, nor were they ever pressured to read sooner than they were ready.

The actual process of natural reading takes years. Learning to read wasn't something that had any kind of time-frame. The process was natural, and evolved over time.

I read to all of my kids since they were in the womb. I read them chapter books and short stories. We had board books and activity books, nature books, science experiment books, and everything else in-between. Our bookshelves overfloweth!

We subscribe to magazines based on their interests and passions. Our family is surrounded by the written word. Learning through immersion is one way in which Unschoolers learn to read naturally.

The ages at which my children learned to read are hard to pin down, as it was such natural process, much like learning to talk. It happened slowly, over time.

Devin, Tiffany, Ivy, and Orion all know how to read now, and I look back on their individual processes as a beautiful time in our lives.

I will never tire of hearing, "Mom! How do you spell the word, 'circumstance'?" or "Mom, what is this word – r-e-n-d-e-z-v-o-u-s?"

I will forever cherish the years in which they all learned the tool that is used to bring such joy and expansion to their lives.

Being that they all learned later than children in school, the first books that they chose to read were based on their interests, and not books they were forced to work through because of a curriculum or age recommendation.

The first book that Ivy read was, "The Long Hard Road Out Of Hell" by Marilyn Manson. Ivy enjoyed hearing about Marilyn Manson's childhood, and his life journey to get to where he is today. This book is not something you'd envision to be a child's first book, that's for sure.

I did a lot of research before buying it for her, and had some serious discussions with Devin, Bonnie, and Ivy before she read it. (Bonnie had read it before and knew that some of the content was intense and sexually focused).

I have had conversations with Ivy about what the book is about, as Marilyn Manson had a unique and cringe-worthy childhood in many areas of his life. The book is also powerfully inspiring. It's compelling to hear about how he went from an unpopular freak (when he was in school) to the captivating rockstar he is now. Supporting Ivy in choosing this book was a journey, but in the end, I am so glad that I did the inner work necessary to support her, instead of forbidding her.

. . .

R adical Unschooling isn't a journey for the faint of heart. It isn't a role for a parent who is fearful, or who isn't willing to dig into the deepest parts of their soul, and do the inner work necessary to heal from your past.

Being able to support my children in their choices, even when they push my personal boundaries, is something that I have worked on diligently. I try not be triggered by my own issues when something intense or controversial comes up in our lives.

Facilitating a life of freedom for my children hasn't been easy, but it's been worth every moment with them. Living a life by their side, helping them learn and grow, has been such an incredible journey. Being judged, criticized, laughed at, shamed, and even threatened has just been part of my life of living-out-loud, standing behind my children's choices, and their rights.

Never in a million years would I have thought that my sweet little daughter's first book would be Marilyn Manson's autobiography, but here I am – standing on the edge of this incredible experiment of giving a child freedom and respect. Thanks for coming along on our journey.

CHAPTER 26

WHY UNSCHOOLING DOESN'T COME NATURALLY

A question keeps popping into my head; if I lived on a deserted island, and had no cultural influence telling me what to do, would unschooling come completely naturally to me as a parent? Why do we need, in order to learn how to unschool in our culture? If it is such a natural way for humans to learn, why do so many people think learning has to be forced?

As I ponder these thoughts, I realize most in our culture have lost instinctual wisdom as parents. We have lost an aspect of being human that is our birthright.

Most people today have never been given the opportunity to be authentic, pure, and whole parents, simply because of what we are born into.

We begin our relationships in a culture that insists an invisible barrier be placed between ourselves and our children. We have been plagued with ignorant advice and ideas, generation after generation.

Giving birth in our culture is more like buying a product, or adopting a pet. The fact a baby is a human is never really impressed upon us, or focused on. We have been so far removed from the natural process that instead of well-wishes, we receive warnings, like the tags on electrical appliances, from the moment our babies are born.

Some of the popular warnings for parents today are:

- Do not be too kind to your children, because you will seem weak, and they will walk all over you.
- Do not give them too much, or you will make them greedy and materialistic.
- Do not let them sleep with you at night, or you will ruin their chances of ever sleeping by themselves.
- Do not hold or touch them too much or you will make them too clingy.
- Make them go to school and obey, or they will never learn.
- Do not allow a child to choose, because they will make bad choices.

Unfortunately, these unfounded beliefs are so ingrained in who we are as a culture, they are the strongest messages parents receive from the beginning. All of these instructions take away the joy, authenticity, and purity from our relationship with our children.

Today's parenting advice is so distancing, it is more like instructions for *parenting-lite* than truly parenting. We are a society controlled by the opinions and advice of others, instead of looking deep within ourselves to find answers.

As a natural childbirth educator, I am regularly asked, "If birth is so natural, why do we need a class?"

My response is that birth has been taken away from women. We have disempowered women so much that we have lost the inner wisdom and confidence it takes to birth naturally. Our culture has changed what birth truly is for women, and their babies. Because of this fact, rather than passing down empowerment, we pass down fear through the ages.Our inner wisdom is still there.

I believe that the same warping has happened with our children, and their ability to learn independently. The joy and ease of natural learning has been stolen from children, and so has the confidence that parents are supposed to have for them to learn. With this insight, I have come to realize that we have to undo so much to get back to the primitive, instinctual wisdom that we all have deep down. It is still there! We just have to slough off all of our cultural armor to get to it.

Our inner wisdom is still there. It is there, underneath all the warnings, and the have-to's. Underneath all of the fear. Underneath all of the self-doubt. Together, we can learn how to remove all of the cultural armor slowly placed upon us growing up. In order to do this, we must support one another on our journey to a more peaceful, authentic way of life. We can invite our true nature, that has been crushed down, to reveal itself.

First, we must be willing to allow ourselves to do something our culture is unaccustomed to, and that is to *trust ourselves and our children*. We can remove our armor, and stand vulnerable before each other. We can learn to redress our spirit with a new mindset. We are not alone! We can go through this journey together, and wrap one another with silk ribbons of ~ love ~ trust ~ kindness ~ joy ~ and ~ appreciation ~ for ourselves, and for our children. We can relight our own flames of instinctual wisdom, and begin again.

CHAPTER 27

RADICAL UNSCHOOLING: THE GIFT OF MINDFULNESS

Radical Unschooling is a very present-based philosophy. The focus of our life is on happiness, and pursuing our interests with reckless abandon, together. We totally immerse ourselves in our passions every single day, and we do so in the *now*.

Children very naturally live in the present, so living this philosophy feels good and right to them. They rarely worry about the future in the way most adults in our culture do. In fact, they do not understand the constant preparation that kids in school are forced to live every day.

It's interesting to me that our culture *constantly* puts a focus on our children's future.

Our kids are trained from toddlerhood to live in the space of preparation, instead of enjoying the moment. Then, we spend years as adults trying to *undo* this conventional mindset through yoga, meditation and self-help books to convert us *back* to our natural way of being, which is to be more present and living in the Now.

I feel that **Radical Unschooling** is the most natural, *zen* way for children to live – for anyone to live, for that matter!

When we never take this default way of being mindful away from children, they never have to go through all that so many of us have to as adults, just to get back to the state of *being* that feels so good, and so fulfilling.

It is so important to notice when we are rushing kids through their daily experiences, just to get to the *next thing on the list.*

Are we rushing them through dinner to get their bath done?

Are we rushing through their bedtime story to get them to bed on time?

Are we rushing (and planning) our lives with our children away, all for the sake of a schedule?

Our children know when our agenda, or schedule, is more important to us than they are in the moment. This deeply affects our connection with them. If we are feeling rushed through our daily routine when we are interacting with our kids, it may be a good time to reflect on what is important in life.

The house can wait. Our email can wait. Our to-do list should never come before modeling mindfulness, and putting everything aside for our children in the moment.

You do have to have a great deal of trust, living in the present. It has taken me some time to allow things to *just flow* for our family, from day to day.

Once a year, our state requests evaluations of our children's progress. It is during this time when I do a lot of reflecting, and writing about all my children have done as Unschoolers.

Amazingly (to those living a conventional life), our children learn and progress far more than children in school, even from an academic perspective. We never 'teach' them the traditional subjects taught in schools, yet they learn reading, writing, math, science, history and so much more, just as a side effect of living their bliss in the present moment, every single day!

Our children have a depth of happiness and self-worth that I did not know until I was an adult, just through having the freedom to be present and mindful.

Through **Radical Unschooling**, we never take away the natural born state of simply *being* from them. Their inner guidance is respected, trusted, and never silenced by my worry about their future.

Does this sound neglectful, or *mindful?*

I know in my heart that that happy moments lead to happy days, happy weeks, happy months, and happy years.

A joyful, fulfilling life overflowing with self-love is the result of a childhood pure and unfettered by someone else's future-based agenda.

Being mindful isn't something our kids will ever have to learn in the way that most of us do today. By keeping our focus on happiness, connection, mindfulness, and love, we give our children the greatest gift that they could ever receive – their *wholeness.*

CHAPTER 28

UNSCHOOLING MUSIC

Living an Unschooling life, we strive to give our children as big a world as possible to learn and grow from. One aspect in which we do this, is surrounding our children with a variety of music, and musical instruments. We have so many instruments in our Unschooling home. We have a drum set, accordion, guitars, recorders, xylophone, Chinese Flute, harmonicas, an ocarina, didgeridoos, and many other fun and exciting tools for their interest in music. We also have a variety of music playing in our home often, from classical, to heavy metal, and everything in between!

We recently acquired a piano from a friend who was moving. From the moment Devin sat down in front of it, he began playing. I mean *really* playing, beautifully!

When a child shows a gift for something, the parent is often pushed to put that child in some kind of class. However, our Unschooled children rarely have an interest in taking lessons at all, and it isn't something I would ever coerce, bribe, or encourage them to do. I would simply give it as an option.

It's easy to slip into that future-based mindset of thinking your child may become a professional musician or dancer someday, just because they show a talent or passion for something.

On the Unschooling path, which is a very present and in-the-moment way of living, it is helpful for parents to not get sucked into the culturally common practice of lessons being the *only* way for personal expansion and growth.

There are many ways in which you can support your child on their musical path. One way is to just *be* there! Listen to the music they create, and be present with them in their passion.

At this point in his life, Devin has no interest in music lessons. When his Unschooled friends come over, they create music together, and record videos. He truly enjoys the experience of playing in his own way. His music is so unique, so beautiful, and perfectly *him*. I would never want to rob that from him, by having a piano teacher tell him how (and what) he should be playing, pulling him from his instinctual connection to the music he loves so much.

I love the foundation of support and trust we create for our children by living a Radical Unschooling life.

We never have to rely on teachers or professionals to perfect our children's skills and talents, even in such areas as music. All of my kids will continue on their own paths of musical growth, in the way they choose to.

Musical talent isn't something that has to be 'taught'. It is something inside those who choose to allow it to grow.

We, as Unschooling parents, can choose to bring as much of the musical world into our children's lives as possible to choose from, and, if an interest or passion grows as a result, we can continue to nurture it with loving support, choices, and options.

CHAPTER 29

UNSCHOOLING AND SELF-WORTH

We take it from our children starting in preschool, then, once they hit their teen years, we start trying to give it back to them. We see that the spark that they once had, is missing.

It's their self-love, and inner knowing.

The institution of traditional parenting is set up in such a way that parents end up believing they need to help instil self-worth into children. It seems a prevalent idea, that self-esteem and confidence are things that need to be *gained* or *built.*

Our Unschooled children, who are growing up in a partnership paradigm, never lose the self-worth that all humans are naturally **born with.**

. . .

From the moment we come into this world, our default setting is to love ourselves. It is all part of human survival. You do not see an animal in the wild feeling insecure, or living with low self-esteem. It isn't something that needs to be gained, or instilled in children, unless kids are robbed of it through living a life where others value obedience and conformity above a child's own needs and desires.

In the old paradigm, parents and educators *create* the very problems they are trying to *fix*. In the same way a doctor's preventative actions oftentimes cause problems in birth, the current parenting model creates low self-esteem and insecurity, that it later tries to fix. Then, it seems the institution is actually to *thank* for their child feeling better about themselves! How twisted is that? The traditional role of the parent and/or educator is what caused the child to lose their inner knowing, and self-love, to begin with! How much work we create for ourselves as a culture, when all we have to do, is shift in how we are doing things.

The authoritarian paradigm is *old school!*

A partnership paradigm is natural, organic, and

authentic. This philosophy is on the leading edge of thought.

More and more parents are waking up to see the reality of all they are creating in their children through parenting from the old model. Haven't we learned how damaging it is to demand obedience, and use punishments and rewards to control another human being? There is another way, and it is called *Radical Unschooling.*

When we live our lives in the new paradigm, kids never lose their inner knowing of *who they are.* They do not need to rely on others *telling* them about their greatness, to *know* about their greatness.

I find it fascinating that my children do not care what others think about them. This *doesn't* mean that they don't care about others' feelings, or needs. On the contrary, my children have a great deal of empathy for others. They just don't value what others think of them as being any reflection of how they measure their own self-worth.

Children love themselves *unconditionally* when they are loved without condition.

This is the power of partnership, connection, and Unschooling!

CHAPTER 30

MATH – UNSCHOOLING STYLE

U nschooling is a free-flowing experience. It takes trust on several levels, but in one way, it means to truly believe the idea that learning and life are not separate. It is knowing that your children will learn the basics through living a life with many resources, and unwavering parental support, love, and involvement.

Last night, the kids really wanted to go out to dinner to Friendly's. It is their favorite place to go for dinner, and they *always* get the same thing. I shared with them that we only had half the spending money it normally costs us to eat out there. I offered a few options to make it possible. I jumped online. and found a coupon. It was, *buy one adult dinner, and get a kid's meal free*. Cool! There is one meal free!

I asked the girls if they minded giving Orion one quarter of their meals each. I showed the girls what I meant by *one quarter* by drawing graphs, and explaining how much of their meal they would be sharing with Orion. Tiff then drew a graph herself, and exclaimed that Orion would have *half* a meal if they each shared a quarter of theirs, and half was perfect for him! The graphs were helpful tools to her in that moment, and I was there to share useful information with her.

Unschooled kids *do* learn math, but in a way that isn't linear. It is in bits and pieces when needed.

My kids have learned math when they have actually needed it in their lives. These bits and pieces are like drops in a puddle that slowly grow to form a very broad and balanced education throughout the childhood years.

When we are here as parents, offering tools and resources, our kids are receptive. They truly desire the support and information we share with them.

It turned out that buying only three meals (with a fourth meal being the free kids meal) was plenty for our family of six. We were able to meet the needs of everyone in the family through discussion, and figuring out a way to make it work.

When money is an issue, most people tend to

think in an *either/or* mentality, especially when they think they can't afford something. I've learned that by shifting to possibility, options are created.

When a child uses math as a tool to understand the world around them, it is learned easily and precisely. When learned in context with their own real life experiences, it goes from being something that is *hard* to learn, to *a cool way to figure something out.*

My children never have to memorize the times tables. They do, however, understand, and use, multiplication and fractions as tools to get more of what they want in life.

Internal motivation is the key to true learning.

Memorization is not learning. In fact, it takes up the precious space of thoughts and desire of the person being forced to memorize.

Think of the unique, rich, tapestry of the uncontrolled mind! This is, to me, a level of freedom and respect that all humans deserve, but rarely get to experience.

A traditional education is like handing a child a paint-by-numbers project, while standing over their shoulder, commenting on their work. It feels safe, and you think you know how it will turn out.

. . .

L iving an Unschooling life is like handing a child a blank canvas, which you create together, whilst listening to the sound of beautiful music in the background. This lifestyle is peaceful, creative, connected, unique, and perfectly individualized.

With Unschooling, true human potential thrives.

CHAPTER 31

UNSCHOOLING CHORES

My Unschooled children have never had chores. We have never had charts hanging on our fridge, with certain household tasks for them to take care of, with stickers as rewards. Yet, Devin, Tiff, Ivy and Orion all help with the housework because they truly *want* to. How is this possible?

When I clean, and do the little tasks I find necessary to keep our house organized throughout the day, I do so *joyfully*. I never slam things around, or get frustrated that toys are on the floor, or that dishes are in the sink. I don't huff and puff, and talk under my breath about being everyone's *slave*. Who would want to help if I was complaining about cleaning all the time?

I truly feel *gratitude* in my heart every time I

clean, or pick something up, because I feel such love and happiness for having my family, and for all that comes with having children.

I see the little scraps of paper on the floor, or books strewn about, and remember the story behind them. I see the craft project Ivy did, or the books I read to Tiff, and see how much they enjoyed our time together, cuddled on the couch.

I pick up, or clean, whatever needs to be done in the moment, unconditionally, and with love. I bask in the gratitude of our life together, without resenting the messes my children make.

I value my relationships, and my connection with my children, over the cleanliness of our home.

Some parents think they have no choice but to coerce, reward, or force children to do chores to instil a sense of responsibility. I feel very differently about this. I feel that my children will naturally be responsible, when they feel a partnership in our family.

Our home is their nest. It is a place they feel is theirs, as much as it is mine. They love their home! They see cleaning as something we do that makes sense. Radical Unschooling creates responsible children in a kind, loving, positive way. When children are respected and trusted, they naturally step into the roles many parents today force their children into, only to create angry, rebellious children and teens.

You never have to force, punish, or manipulate a child into helping with the housework. You only have to clean joyfully, and set the base standard for how you want your home to be. Your children will naturally assist in maintaining the standard by which they are used to living, and they will do so in a way that feels meaningful to them.

Model joy and gratitude surrounding housework, but do so authentically. You can't fake it, in an attempt to manipulate your children into helping out. Children always know your true feelings, and sense the intent behind your actions.

Last night, my children were cleaning until almost midnight! Ivy and Orion washed windows, and cleaned inside the fridge. Devin mopped the floors, and Tiff vacuumed the whole house, including the stairs!

It was a fun night of housework, with music playing loudly in the background. No power struggles. No threats. No punishments, or tears. Just pure connection and authentic fun as we cleaned our home together – in joy and gratitude.

CHAPTER 32

UNSCHOOLING FOOD FREEDOM

I t might shock some people that my children can choose whatever they want from the supermarket, just like I do.

Our financial limits vary from month to month, but within our budget, they have the freedom to choose whatever they want for snacks and meals. They will very often take their own cart, and just go off and shop for themselves. I love this aspect of the Radical Unschooling life!

Honesty and balance are important values to me in the relationship with my children. During a recent interview about Unschooling, the interviewer told me that her child once wanted some candy at the store. She suggested an apple, and told her child he would get sick if he ate the candy. Personally, I would never say something that was untrue, or exaggerated, as a means to control children with fear to sway them in their choices. It isn't in alignment with Radical Unschooling philosophy.

For my kids, some candy would *not* make them sick. In fact, if I said that to them, and they ate it, and did *not* get sick, how would that affect the trust between us in the future? I know they wouldn't take what I said as truth very much after that, knowing that the information I was giving them was false, and a means of control.

I believe that any foods, in moderation, are fine for our bodies. I know there are people with allergies, and food intolerances, and I am not talking about those people here. I know there are exceptions to everything.

Right now, I am sharing about *my* children, who are healthy, happy, and thriving; who have real freedom with the foods that they choose to put in their bodies.

What is interesting to me, about how some parents process freedom surrounding foods, is that they tend to think in extremes, with fear as the backdrop. If children have been controlled by food restrictions in the past, and these restrictions are suddenly lifted, the natural response is overindulgence with the foods that *were* taboo. These children do not know when, and if, the restrictions will be reinstated, so they get as much as they can, struggling for their own autonomy.

A grocery cart filled with candy, cakes, soda, and chips would (more than likely) be their choice. This image is what most in our culture think of, when they think of Unschoolers with food freedom. In our experience, with four Radical Unschooling children with food freedom, this is not the case at all!

Children raised with the Radical Unschooling philosophy, who have true food freedom, make very different choices than the average child. Just like you and I have the freedom to choose what we eat, and we *do not* fill our carts with candy, cakes, chips, and soda, neither do children with *true food freedom.*

When Unschooled kids are allowed to tap into their own inner knowing and bodily cravings, and they know about their bodies and what nourishes them, they can make choices in what they are drawn to. I believe this is the healthiest, most organic way to raise my children surrounding food.

A healthy, balanced person with freedom to choose does *not* make unhealthy choices. It wouldn't make sense to my kids not to eat a balanced, healthy diet. They love and respect their bodies. They crave and desire fruits, veggies, nuts, grains, protein, and sugars.

Another important thing I would like to share, is that I do not blame my children's behavior on certain ingredients in foods, like so many parents in our culture do. So much is blamed on foods, and I believe this attitude is so unhealthy for the parent/child relationship. I feel that the parents aren't taking responsibility for their role in their children's behavior, and are using foods as a *catch-all blame bucket*. Parents today are desperately trying to control what their kids eat, in an attempt to control *them*. A more respectful way to parent, in my eyes, would be to focus on the needs under a child's behavior, instead of trying to control behavior with food restrictions and limits.

Honesty and trust are paramount to a Radical Unschooling life, and to a child having a healthy, balanced relationship with food. I do not have fear surrounding certain foods, like many people in our culture do. There is nothing off-limits to my family. The entire grocery store is our buffet, and we choose without limiting ourselves. We love farmer's markets, and we have a large garden that the kids help, with and enjoy. We love food, and trust our bodies.

I think coming to this place in life (surrounding food, and how I respect my kids choices) is a combination of things. It is my personal belief, surrounding my body, and the foods I put in it. It is the trust I have of my children's choices. I give them information about food, and my children have the freedom to choose what they want based on their knowledge, and what they are craving.

I think when people envision Unschooling, and children having food freedom, they are basing their image on the distrustful, disrespectful ideas that most people have of children's choices.

Most people have never witnessed *truly free children*.

They are basing their beliefs on children with limits which may have been (temporarily) lifted. Kids are often looked at as not being capable, or experienced enough, to know what is good for them, and what isn't.

I believe children are so much closer to achieving balance then adults are, because of the fearful mixed-messages (and conflicting ideas) surrounding food in our society, that we have been conditioned with.

CHAPTER 33

FREEDOM IS NOT UNPARENTING!

F reedom does not mean un-involvement in a child's life. That is neglect. Freedom is choices, respect, and honoring each person's individual path with connected support, love, and nurturing. This is at the heart of Radical Unschooling!

Oftentimes, when I am working with parents who are learning about Unschooling, they share what isn't working for them from their parenting tool box. They share that punishments aren't working, and comment on how damaging they are for the parent/child relationship.

When a parent knows what they do *not* want to do, but has no idea what *to* do (in place of punishments) they sometimes feel like Unschooling is not doing anything at all. Nothing could be further from the truth!

Radical Unschooling is a very hands-on approach, and it is *not un-parenting!* Unschooling is certainly not for the lazy parent! Rules and punishments are very easy in comparison to how we choose to live our lives in partnership with our children through Radical Unschooling.

Shifting from control to connection takes patience, love, and a willingness to rethink everything you thought you knew. It takes courage to see there is another way – a better way to raise children!

Unschooling is the greatest gift a parent could ever give a child, and I am so grateful to be walking this amazing path, hand in hand with my children!

CHAPTER 34

LIST OF WHAT NOT TO DO
WHEN YOU HAVE A BABY

IF YOU GENUINELY VALUE THEIR FREEDOM

1 **Don't birth in a hospital.**
Only 1% of women need to birth in a
hospital for true medical necessity. Birth is big business, and the intention to undermine your ability (for profit) is immense. Home-birth is much safer than birthing in a hospital, because your ability to birth, and parent your child, will not be undermined by those who wish to sever that bond from the beginning.

2 **Don't buy the many useless baby items they try to sell you.**
A baby carrier is all you truly need, and is all your baby wants. Your presence is something that

creates a connection with your child. This bond is not something that the government and corporations want. Tools of disconnection will be marketed to you.

3 Don't formula feed.

Mothers' milk is a living fluid, like blood. This can never be duplicated in a factory. It's a billion dollar business, and believe me when I say that hospitals are in on it! They get kickbacks if they undermine breastfeeding, so you have to buy formula. Sick babies (from denial of breastmilk) create sick and dependent humans.

4 Don't use a crib.

Co-sleeping is what humans are born to do. Cribs, and letting a baby cry it out, are ways in which mothers slowly, but positively, silence their inner voice to be able to respond to their babies needs.

When we are taught to ignore our babies' cries, this learned helplessness is something a human carries with them through most of their lives. Mothers then lose the ability to tune into inner wisdom. As a result, they are left needing to rely on 'experts' to tell them how to mother. This is all perfectly orchestrated by those who wish to sever the parent-child bond, to gain control and influence.

Sadly, our culture drugs children when they don't focus on what adults want them to be focused on. Yet, our culture also condemns children, if they are focused on something they enjoy.

The child, judged as being in a *zombie-like-state*, is a child so engrossed in what they are doing, that they block out everything else around them. They are in a zen-like state of focus, but when a parent fears something, or if a parent is annoyed at the child (perceivably) ignoring them, a child's focus on what they are doing is annoying to the parent.

So, is drugging kids *really* about helping them to focus? Or is it about making it easier to force a child to submit to the control of adults? It is inhumane to attempt to force focus on anyone, just because you think it is best for them. Lack of focus and/or attention isn't a disorder. It is simply a lack of interest.

It's time we wake up to the hypocrisy (and double-standards) our culture promotes.

Open your heart to see the goodness in your child, and the beauty and perfection in their interests. Celebrate their natural focus.

~

5 Don't put your children in school.

Indoctrination is the final way in which the government (and all connected to it) want to control the minds of young people, telling them what to think and believe. Once your children are entirely disconnected from you, they are so easy to mold into what the state wants them to be - unhealthy consumers, who depend on others for everything.

Keeping society dumbed down is the goal. Making kids believe they are learning and achieving is all an illusion. It is a form of control parents buy into, because their ability to raise their children has been undermined from the very beginning of life. When a mother loses her ability to birth, feed, intuitively parent, and nurture, *of course* they will also rely on the government to educate.

Creating disconnection, undermining inner wisdom, silencing intuition, cultivating consumerism, and, finally, creating fear and dependence, is what governments want from the moment of birth, in order to own and control people. These ways of disconnecting parents from their children have worked for a very long time – until now.

It's time we wake up to this truth and not be afraid to speak it!

From the beginning of life, patterns are set. We can either become controlled by fear, or we can take it all back. You truly can live a life driven by trust, inner wisdom, and love.

There are many other issues connected with what I share here. I'm happy to hear your voice about whatever this brings up for you. Speaking the truth is essential to empowering others about how to live the freedom every child deserves from the beginning of life.

CHAPTER 35

I'M THAT MOM

You know, that Mom that takes her children sledding at midnight, under the stars, making the neighbors secretly jealous, because they have to sleep to get up early for work and school.

I'm that Mom, who loves to clean and decorate, and who enjoys giving my family a cozy, joyful place to call their nest. I express my creativity using my home as my canvas. I want *home* to be a place my children love to be; where they feel safe, happy, and inspired.

I'm that Mom, who always assumes positive intent from my children, and sees them as fully capable people.

I'm that Mom, who encourages my children to

explore their own beliefs, even when they differ from my own.

I'm that Mom, who enjoys the music my children love, and who turns up the volume (as loudly as they want) in the car.

I am that Mom, who loves bands like Metallica and Slayer, and who still dives into mosh pits at their concerts.

I'm that Mom, who kisses the mirror and says, "I love you," to myself while my children are watching.

I'm that Mom, who explores my own interests fully, with reckless abandon, inspiring my children (through my passion) to learn more about what I am into.

I'm that Mom, who oftentimes makes a different meal for everyone in the family. I trust that whatever they are craving is exactly what their bodies need, yet I don't feel like a *"short-order cook, a waitress or a slave."* I feel like a nurturing *mother*.

I'm that Mom, who chooses to be my children's voice if they are in a situation where they are uncomfortable, or unable to express their feelings or needs.

I'm that Mom, who sometimes pays for the coffee, or a toll for the person in the car behind us, just for the joy of it. My children love practicing random acts of kindness with strangers.

I'm that Mom, who no longer has babies or toddlers who are physically dependent on me, but who is grateful for the next phase of our lives together as a family. I am rediscovering who I am, now that a decade of pregnancy, nursing and child-wearing is over.

I'm that Mom, who's learning how to paint and make pottery with the encouragement of my children, I'm loving the passion for art and creativity my kids are developing alongside me.

I'm that mom, who keeps her home fully stocked with paint, paper, clay, pastels, and every kind of craft supply imaginable, to fully facilitate our love for creativity.

I'm that Mom, who plays *Grand Theft Auto* with my kids and looks up cheat codes to help them gain access into secret levels of a game that they love. I bring my kids to gaming and Steampunk conventions, and dress up as a character that they created, because they want me to.

I'm that Mom, who will throw towels in the dryer while my children are in the shower, then run them upstairs to surprise them with warm towels on cold, snowy nights.

I'm that Mom, who talks openly and freely about love and sex, and who shares that intimacy is something each of them will learn about in their own time, in their own way. I will be there for them in any way I can to answer questions. I will support them without judgement.

I'm that Mom, who always says, "Yes," when my daughters ask to play with my makeup and beauty products, even when it is my favorite, expensive body wash, because they are worth it to me.

I'm that Mom, who gets a tattoo to represent each of my children. They each pick out a color of their choice to represent them on the tattoo. When other people see my tattoo, they proudly point to which part of the tattoo is 'them'.

I'm that Mom, who will pull out my grandmother's fine china to serve lunch on, as a surprise, to show my family that every day we have together is a special occasion.

I'm that Mom, who makes mistakes sometimes, but who isn't afraid to apologize to my kids. I know that in doing so, they will learn making mistakes is part of learning and growing. They know I am perfectly imperfect.

. . .

I'm exactly the Mom I always wanted to be, despite others telling me it would never happen, because I'd 'know better' once I had my own children.

Yes. I'm *that* Mom.

CHAPTER 36

CULTURAL EVOLUTION

Living a Radical Unschooling life, we focus on our relationships with our children in a way very different from mainstream society.

Almost all of the parenting advice most people receive is about obedience, and controlling children. It is very rare to read about respect, and connection with one's children.

Partnership parenting is at the heart of Unschooling. This life is about living a completely different paradigm than the one most of us were raised in. The authoritarian paradigm is the only dynamic most know about. However, once people hear the logic of partnership parenting through Radical Unschooling, they are brought to a new level of awareness about the respect, love, and kindness that is terribly lacking in our culture, in regards to children.

Radical Unschooling truly is an evolution in how children are viewed in our society. We have evolved an acceptance of others, in many other ways, in our culture; children are next on the agenda. They are deserving of equal rights and respect.

I am honored to help lead the way in raising awareness about this incredibly important aspect of life with children.

CHAPTER 37

RAISING REBELS: YOUR THOUGHT FOR THE DAY

The most tragic lesson children learn in school, is how to live in a dictatorship.

The idea of quitting something doesn't exist in our lives, because a child will complete as much as they want of a topic until they are personally satisfied. When they've gained enough knowledge or information that meets their own needs, they move on. Our children's work doesn't have to be finished, or completed, according to someone else's standards.

U nschooled kids can go as far as they can understand or desire. This aspect of natural learning is different than in a forced learning situation, where children are not only made to finish things, but are also graded on how well they do. The focus when it comes to learning, is not on content, but on compliance, and obedience.

W e respect our children on their own paths in what they want to know in life. Humans learn best when they are internally motivated. When children are driven by their own desires they learn what they need to, and it will not be according to someone else's idea of what is best for them.

L earning is pleasurable when it isn't forced. Self-worth and confidence are stolen from children, starting in toddlerhood, and once they start preschool. Then, once they hit their teen years, we try to hammer it back into them, wondering how it was lost so early on. We see that the spark that they once had is now missing. We realize something went terribly wrong, and that the joyful, once-confident child, filled with self-love and beauty, is now insecure, unsure of themselves, and fearful.

The institutions of traditional parenting and forced schooling are set up in such a way that the common authoritarian practices of control and punishment actually rob children of what they were born with - self love, and a healthy level of self-esteem.

What we don't see are adults realizing that it is *they* who cause their child's breakdown of self-love and confidence to begin, through common parenting practices of behavior modification and punishment.Our culture blames TV, music, video games, and phones, further fearing parents to control and limit these things. This causes a crumbling of a child's inner knowing and further damages them by taking away more of the child's tools for self-expression and freedom.

When you raise children in a peaceful, partnership-based paradigm, they rarely lose the self-worth and self love that all humans are naturally born with. From the moment we come into this world, our default setting is to love ourselves. It is part of human survival.

You do not see an animal in the wild insecure, or living with low self-esteem. It isn't something that needs to be gained, or instilled in children, unless they are robbed of it through living a life where others value obedience and conformity above a child's own needs and desires.

We all want to be loved. We all want to be safe. We all want to be free. We are one.

You could never force a child to truly respect you. If you think respect means obedience, you are an oppressor. Oppressors are never truly respected - they are simply feared.

Demanding that you be respected by your children while treating them disrespectfully will only result in their resentment of you - which will grow exponentially over time.

Once they are adults and you grow old, if they decide to put you in a nursing home instead of caring for you, this truth will become more clear. Respect your children. Treat them the way you hope they will treat you someday, when they are all you have left.

The precious and sacred space in our children's minds doesn't need to be filled with pointless, mind-numbing information that has no purpose, or use to them, in a real-life context. Instead, they should have the freedom to ignite the fire of passionate learning through living a life of their choosing, and doing what they enjoy with their time, instead of living the agenda of others. Learning will happen in real and powerful ways, despite your fears.

Freedom of mind is an often overlooked aspect of children's rights, because we think we know better than they do. However, a child's desire for freedom is a natural force within them that drives their very being each and every day. The more we deny them this freedom, through forced learning, the more it warps who they are, and who they become.

The idea that our children should be filling their minds like sand in a bottle, with all the grains representing memorised information, is a flawed practice. Instead, we can choose to smash that bottle, and expand their capacity to learn and grow, by respecting their autonomy and freedom of mind.

The resources for learning are endless, and can't be contained. Our children will learn and grow in ways that we never knew were possible. We are the ones who should be open to learning from them, as they are much more graceful learners than we were ever allowed to be.

I know that our culture rushes children to grow up too quickly. Parents are told that if you don't force your children to be independent, they never will be. Nothing could be further from the truth!

Children whose dependant needs are met, grow into independence as strong, confident, and whole people, compared to children who have had their needs ignored because an expert said they should be more independent at an arbitrary age.

An unmet need doesn't just go away because a parent refuses to meet it. The unmet needs warps into dysfunction, that forms their personality, and their ability to connect and trust other people.

Treat your children like prophets and geniuses, because they are.

It's interesting to me that our culture constantly puts a focus on children's futures. Young people are trained from toddlerhood to live in the space of preparation, instead of enjoying being *in the moment*.

Then, we spend years as adults trying to undo this conventional mindset, through yoga, meditation, and self- help books, to convert us back to our once-natural way of living in mindful presence.

To nurture this way of being it is important to notice when we are rushing kids through their daily experiences, just to get to the next thing on the list. Are we rushing them through dinner to get their bath done? Are we rushing through their bedtime story to get them to bed on time? Are we rushing, and planning, their childhood away, as if parenting them in itself was simply a task to get through every day?

Our children know when our agenda or schedule is more important to us than their needs. When we put this before them, it deeply affects our relationship with them, and a disconnect begins. If we are feeling stressed by our daily routine with our children, it may be a good time to reflect on what is truly important in life. The house can wait. Our email and social media can wait. Our desire to check things off of our to-do list should never come before our children's need for the freedom to truly live in the present moment.

The inner work necessary to truly accept this way of living with your children isn't easy. It is common for parents to take the position of their childhood abuse, trauma, fear, and control as having been necessary.

Many parents, especially fathers, feel they wouldn't be the strong men they are today without having been parented punitively. Accepting another way would mean they need to face the fact they never had to be punished or controlled to become good people.

When we accept there is a more peaceful, loving and respectful way to raise children, we then have to accept that the way many of us were parented was often damaging, and has caused issues in our lives that we are still working on today. Not everyone is ready to take all of that on.

The choice to live in a peaceful, freedom-based paradigm with children requires diligent inner work, personal growth, and healing. Meeting the needs of everyone in the family equally takes time and patience. I love that so many parents are accepting there is a better way to raise children than the way most of us were parented. This is where peace, and healing of the world, begins.

Parents today are trained through subtle fear tactics to raise their children to get used to being controlled by authority. It is in the best interests, of those who want to rule us, that our children be groomed to be subservient into adulthood.

Do not believe for a moment that the current parenting paradigm of control is what is best for your children. If you do, you've been duped, and are only being used as a tool to help make the government's job easier.

When we realize this, we can reject the current cultural training of parents, and step into a greater awareness of what our children truly need from us.

Children do not need to be controlled. They need freedom, kindness, respect, love and most of all - our presence.

The manipulation of us as parents has been going on for so long, our culture has accepted it as *normal* to control and train children to submit to authority.

It is one of the greatest cons in human history. We must wake up, and see this truth, for a more peaceful and loving world.

"This will hurt me more than it hurts you. I'm punishing you because I love you."

From the beginning, we were conditioned to think those who ruled over us, cared about us. We were brainwashed to believe that authority plus control equals love.

Most parents today still believe the only way to truly love their child, is to control and punish them. If they didn't, the truth of their childhood would be staring back at them, beneath the manipulation and lies. It's not an easy reality to step into.

Most parents can't accept the life of freedom and peace with children that I promote, because the memories of their childhood could alter and morph into darkness in the acceptance of it. Not everyone is ready to take on that level of pain, and heal enough to live this life.

Just because your kids *can* do something on their own, doesn't mean you should never do it for them. Ivy and Orion said that food tastes *so* good when I bring it to them while they are playing Minecraft on the computer. Folding Devin's clothes isn't something I *have* to do. He is happy doing it himself, but I know he appreciates the thought when I bring him a neat pile of clothes, and put it on his bed. When he smiles, and looks at me, and says, "Thanks, Mom," I know it is something he is learning from, and truly appreciates.

When you love someone, you do nice things for them –even if they are capable of doing it themselves. Modeling loving kindness is just as important of a responsibility to me, as a mother, as encouraging them to do things on their own.

Don't be afraid to be kind to your children! How else will they learn to be kind to others?

As children, most of us were controlled and abused by the adults in our lives, even if we were not fully aware of it, because it was happening to every other child we knew.

We were shown that power rules. Punishment, and forced compliance to authority, were at the helm of almost every relationship we had with adults.

A movement of those of us showing a better way - a more peaceful and respectful way - to live with children, is changing the course of history.

This approach is revolutionary, influential, and challenging. It takes re-evaluating our role as parents, and un-brainwashing our minds, which have been conditioned by our own upbringing.

We are in the midst of a complete overhaul of what we once thought parenting was all about. I have faith that many are ready to embrace the idea that children are people, too. They are some of the most discriminated people in our culture today.

We are changing the world through leading the way, and showing others what is possible.

W hen a child looks into my eyes after being scolded or shamed by his parents in public, I feel their plea to be heard. I experience their pain.

I notice that they matter, and that their human dignity falls to the ground, desperately waiting for someone to pick it up off of the floor. I see the discrimination, and the disrespect, they endure.

It's important to remember how this felt for *you* as a child, and connect with those painful memories, to be able to offer the compassion and respect that *you* deserved, with those who need it *now*.

O ften, children need to show their parents the way. If parents could let down their ego long enough to listen, they could learn so much!

Y ou parents, who are brave enough to be called *neglectful* and *lazy* for not using fear, manipulation, control, or punishment as the central focus of your lives and relationship with your children... know you aren't taking the easy path! It takes great strength to focus on the needs of your children, and not merely focus on controlling their behavior.

It takes great confidence to walk with trust and instinct as your guide. It take incredible patience to find ways to parent with peace, honoring the needs of your children with respect.

J ust last night I witnessed this.

I watched as a little child was treated like a dog being trained. I knew their pain. I felt it. No one else seemed to care, or even notice. They looked into my eyes, and I looked deeply into theirs. A tear escaped my eye. I smiled and nodded.

"You're awesome," I whispered.

They smiled back, eyes glossed over, and in those two words, I conveyed the energy of love, understanding, and the acknowledgement that they are worthy of more.

There are many ways to advocate for children. Find your way, and share it with love and confidence. You don't have to be confrontational or loud. You don't need to scream to make a difference. Compassion can be a whisper, a touch, or a smile.

Have no doubt – we are broken! De-conditioning takes years. Finding ourselves beneath it all takes great effort, and inner work. It's a messy, and sometimes scary, experience, but there is no other way to become who we have always wanted to be, and who we would have been long ago, had we not been conditioned to be *something else* to survive.

Our children need to see how we pick up our broken pieces in our lives when we make mistakes - and we will make them! We don't have to hide them anymore, because we think someone will make fun of us, shame us, or punish us.

Now is the time to let down all that we've been forced to build up since childhood, when we needed to protect our sensitive selves.

We need to become what our children need, so they can navigate their world in a healthy, loving and peaceful way.

We need to walk through the fire of our souls, and look deeply at what we need to change within ourselves, and leave a trail of armor behind us. We don't need it anymore, and trust me, your children don't want it either.

Punishing a child turns them unfeeling, angry, and disconnected. It makes their resentment fester under the surface, where it escapes in unusual and destructive ways. You never need to punish. Instead, explain, discuss, share, convey, and connect.

~

Be present and peaceful.

~

Punishments are nothing but bullying and controlling. Children will grow up thinking this is what we do to others who don't do what we want. Elevate, evolve, and take the time to model kindness, understanding, and grace. Be the change you want to see in your child.

~

Children are designed to be dependent in a healthy relationship with their parents. It is through meeting their needs fully that children learn how to be independent later on. It is tragic when a parent does not help their child, out of fear that if they do, they will somehow be damaging them, and hindering their growth. In fact, the opposite is true!

~

Children become independent faster when parents let go of fear to connect, support, and assist their kids, when they voice dependent needs. True independence can not be created through neglect.

You do not have to live perfectly, to be the perfect parent, for your children. When we can admit our mistakes, flaws, and issues, we are able to model one of the greatest aspects of being human – the ability to change.

We have to *live* the reality of being human to it's fullest extent, for our children to see what life is truly about. Most of our parents didn't show us much of their inner landscape. They were trained to believe it would be wrong to do so. Our parents, and most parents today, have such crushing pressure to be something they are not, in order to be *good* parents. They are told to become *tough, consistent,* and, essentially, to *withhold love,* through control, punishment, shame, and forced compliance. This is how they teach children to survive in the world.

That way of living with children only benefits those in power. Have no doubt, it hurts parents as much as it does their children, to live together in such an unnatural way.

As parents on the brink of a new paradigm, we need to be brave enough to admit our mistakes. We have to be vulnerable enough for our children to see us cry. We need to be compassionate enough to change our minds when we see another perspective, and we need to be confident enough to become aware of, and heal, our deep inner wounds.

We need to let down the cultural armor we've been forced to build up over the years in order to survive in a broken world. Slowly, with self-love and forgiveness, we can learn to take off our protective armor, piece by piece, knowing we are finally safe, and there is nothing for us to fear anymore.

My need for a clean and organized home does not override my children's needs to use our home as a workshop of their interests. Our kitchen is used as a science laboratory, a place to dye fabric, and and a place to make paper. It's a rollerblading rink. A place to bake, and cook with reckless abandon. A greenhouse, a think tank, and, occasionally, a place to practice yoga handstands.

Right now, our living room is a computer lab, a crafting center, a Bionicle village, a Call of Duty marathon space, a snack-tasting center, a library, a study, and a wrestling arena. Our bathroom is used for not only *washing*, but also for *dyeing* hair red, and as a pet grooming station – among many other messy things.

When I see a mess, I see learning. I see memories being made. I see joy and growth. What I feel, in turn, is deep and powerful gratitude.

When I wake up in the morning and see mess, I think about what the kids made with the materials from the night before, after I went to bed. What is left behind is a story of their creation. Instead of getting pissed off, and huffing obscenities under my breath, I clean up their mess, smile, and feel such love in my heart for having happy, healthy children, who are so creative and passionate about life.

To trust your children, you must first trust yourself.

W hen we threaten freedom in children, they can never truly be whole people. When freedom is threatened, it warps the human condition.

A loving, connected parent who doesn't force, manipulate, or punish a child, has much more influence in a child's life than a parent in an authoritative/authoritarian role.

L iving without punishments (and threats of freedom being lost), children are safer, healthier, and can find true balance in all they do, be it food, sleep, technology, hygiene, their connection to nature, and their relationships.

T he biggest issues parents deal with today are profoundly affected by how our culture tells them to parent. Parents cause the problems, but rarely see how, or why.

An aspect of consciousness that can't be measured by someone else, is a child's attention. Therefore, the idea that a child can be deficient in attention is a complete scam. The treatment of ADD causes more harm than the 'disorder' itself. It's almost unbelievable that a child can be labelled defective, simply because they don't obey, or do what is being forced upon them in school.

Drugging a child is very real form of punishment for disobedience in our culture today. Experimental narco-therapy is a devastating practice, and one with irreversible consequences.Children's brains aren't defective. The entire premise of compulsory institutionalized education is.

Your children need you to be a friend to them. They do not need you to be their boss. Do not dictate, control, punish, judge, or manipulate them out of fear. Be there for them, in the way that they are asking you to be. Facilitate, connect, discuss, love, and be present. Friends trust one another, confide, and listen.

Despite what society tells you, being a friend to a child is the greatest role that you could have in their lives! Don't be controlled by fear of what will happen if you do this. It is all a lie to control you! Wake up and smell the agenda, and the intent of those who perpetuate this belief! Your children *need you* to be their greatest friend. Do this, and your relationship with your child will improve in wondrous ways!

When a child is friends with their parents, they trust their parents. They confide. They listen. They believe the information we give them. They have no reason to fear us. When you have a deep bond and connection, you are of great influence in their lives. This is what the role of a parent should be, and one that you can have, if you let go of the fear-based, culturally-perpetuated, ideas surrounding this.

We spent our childhood years crying it out, only to be ignored. We were told it was necessary, for us to learn we aren't the center of the Universe. Sadly, this common tactic backfired, and made us toxic, needy, overly dependent, and fearful. We felt invisible to everyone around us. Now, we spend our lives in a state of demanding, bullying, and forcing others – to see us, to listen to us, to respects us – only to have that backfire as well.

The entire premise of *tough love* has proven itself to be false over and over again, yet it's still promoted as being essential for 'teaching' a child how to be independent. It models the opposite, but sadly, we still live in the do-as-I-say-not-as-I-do mentality, even though it's proven itself wrong, time and time again.

It can be abundantly difficult for parents raised in an authoritarian paradigm to let go of fear of their own needs not being met, long enough to meet the needs of their children. Authoritarian parenting is a fear-based approach. Therefore, control is the first (and ongoing) thread of energy in that type of relationship between parent and child.

It is only through helping a parent heal from their own upbringing that we can encourage and support a parent enough to let go of unhealthy, damaging tactics such as yelling, shaming, and blaming.

In order for us to help our children, we have to help the parent, supporting them, as they take a deep look at their own childhood to see that they were abused. When we allow them to see the past (and themselves) with compassion and understanding, the healing process can begin. This is an essential component of stepping into a space of peace and partnership with their own children.

Our culture is so full of hypocrisy, it rarely acknowledges that children are born wired to be dependent. The only way to foster healthy independence, is to meet a child's dependent needs, lovingly and consistently. When a culture starts promoting that ignoring a child's needs is the right way to create independence, we are encouraging abuse as a form of child-rearing. This is devastatingly dangerous for the child, the parent, and the future of our humanity.

Putting convenience first is what everyone today seems to want. With parenting, however, the manipulative way in which this is promoted is not easy to recognize, because when a person is raised having their own needs ignored, they feel they must do the same with their own children, in order to validate their upbringing.

By admitting that a disconnected, detached approach is not healthy, parents are left to face their own issues, and must face that they were, in fact, abused. This isn't something most people are ready for. By repeating history, they never have to face the truth, and their incomplete, damaged selves. Ignorance is bliss, but when you choose ignorance over truth, bliss becomes delusion.

Some of us are here to trigger people. We wake people up. We shake them from their current reality. Our very existence brings them to a deeper understanding of what is possible for a new way of living. However, this isn't always a positive experience for those of us doing the triggering. We often receive a great deal of negative when we choose to live out loud.

It takes massive courage to hold the space to receive this negative energy, and not let it throw you off-balance. One needs to have great focus and clarity about this, while being a voice for change. You *will* trigger the density in others. When you embrace this, you can stop personalizing it, and understand that it is all part of the process in the evolution of human consciousness.

As adults, we relive the patterns we once lived as children. We either become oppressors, because of what was modeled to us, or we stay victims of control and abuse. It is rare that people get out of this way of being in their lifetime, but I've come to realize that the only way in which the world is going to shift towards more peace and compassion, is to reawaken the empathy and compassion that was robbed of us as children.

Punishments and rewards do not work to create nurturing, loving people who care about the needs of others. They actually create people who seek approval, disconnecting them from their internal compass of what feels right to them. Forced obedience to an authority is encouraging narcissism, and modeling this as the ideal way to live.

Children have the human right to own themselves and be motivated by *internal* values of self love, and caring about the needs of others. When they are controlled by fear of *external* threats of punishment, their focus becomes only about self preservation. The ability to focus on others disappears.

If you want self-focused children, who are slowly conditioned not to care about how their behavior affects others, reward and punish them. You'll see how quickly they begin to appear selfish and uncaring because this is what you have modeled to them. If we want to raise compassionate, loving, individuals who care about the needs and feelings of others, it's time to change how we treat them.

Rules are a substitution for being present with children. Like many substitutions, they have risks and negative results.

D o not substitute your presence in your child's life. It is through connection, not control, that children can be joyful, and inspired, and shift the world towards more peace and freedom for future generations.

T he idea that anyone needs to memorize state capitals or times tables is outdated. Forced memorization is an obsolete practice of learning. I suppose it is a branch of learning, where many of us know things from being forced to memorize them. However, I don't consider it necessary, or even healthy. Deeply integrated learning is about internal motivation and desire from the learner. It does not come through force by an authority.

L earning will happen in real and powerful ways, despite your fears!

Freedom of mind is an often overlooked aspect of children's rights, because we think we know better than they do. However, a child's desire for freedom is a natural force within them, that drives their very being, each and every day. The more we deny them this freedom, through forced learning, the more it warps who they are, and who they become.

The idea that our children should be filling their minds, like sand in a bottle, with all of the grains representing memorized information, is a flawed practice. Instead, we can choose to smash that bottle and expand their capacity to learn and grow by respecting their autonomy and freedom of mind. The resources for learning are endless, and can't be contained.

Our children will learn and grow in ways we never knew were possible. We are the ones who should be open to learning from them, as they are much more graceful learners than we were ever allowed to be.

Children are just naturally living in the moment. Our culture feels that they should be constantly preparing for adulthood, yet promotes that adults should be practicing mindfulness and living in the Now. How contradictory this promotion of zen-living is, when children have this conditioned out of them so early on.

We need to stop breaking children of what comes naturally to them, so that they don't spend their adult lives trying to get back to the natural state of *being* that was robbed of them. When we refuse to hand our children over to the state, to raise and educate, we are allowing them not only freedom, but the ability to live joyfully in the moment.

I t takes powerful love to care more about what your children think of you, than what the world thinks of you.

Y our children aren't responsible for making you feel like a good parent. The next time you treat them in a way that you wish you hadn't, and you apologize, don't let it trigger your fear of rejection. You do not need to control them into thinking you're awesome all of the time. It isn't healthy to use them to boost your parenting ego. Your self-worth needs to come from within you.

T he next time you feel the urge to energetically chase your child around after you've made a mistake, pleading to them in various ways, "Love me! Tell me you still love me, and that I am a good, peaceful parent! Don't reject me!" realize how unhealthy that behavior is.

Breathe through the fear. It is damage from your own childhood that is creating your uncontrollable urge to make them soothe you, and make you feel *approved of*. It isn't their job. It is your own childhood wounds that need healing and focus.

Free your children from this burden.

W e do not break life down into subjects; we do not grade, or make our kids do workbook pages, or busy work. We trust that our kids will learn what they need on their own life path to be happy, and in turn, to be successful.

U nschooling has a foundation of trust in children that is virtually unheard of in our culture, because most of us were never trusted as children ourselves.

I respect my children on their own paths in what they want to learn in life. Radical Unschooling is focused on trust, freedom, and the belief that humans learn best when they are internally motivated.

When children are driven by their own desires, they learn what they need to in life, and it is not according to someone else's idea of what is best for them.

We are not all meant to have the same body of knowledge as everyone else. We are all diverse individuals, and our personal knowledge needs to reflect that, for us to reach our full potential in life.

Children in school are all being forced to learn the same dumbed-down content. This is tragic, and entirely driven by those in power who have an overall agenda to control us.

U nschoolers have as much knowledge as any child in school, but it is perfectly catered to who they are as individuals. Their knowledge far exceeds a child in school who has a cookie-cutter experience. My children own their knowledge, and what is in their minds is their business – not mine. One thing that I know for sure - they have a perfectly individualized education, and more importantly, they are living in the freedom and peace that is almost unheard of for children today.

I n order for a child to find balance with something, a parent needs to authentically trust freedom more than they trust control. Only then, will a child have true freedom, and find balance in their lives.

W hen a parent wants to live a life of freedom with their children, they often go through the physical motions of releasing limits on food or technology. However, they still have so much fear and distrust in the process, that their child feels it, and doesn't feel truly free. They worry that their new freedom, with something they love, could be taken away, so they over-consume, as a result. The parent worries, thinking that freedom "doesn't work," and although they've heard of other children finding balance, *their* child must be the exception.

Unfortunately, the parent doesn't realize that it is the energy of fear and control that is causing the over-consumption, not the thing itself!

I explain to parents that what they are living isn't true freedom. I share that a child can only find balance, and gain a healthy relationship with technology and foods, when their parent is living *without* fear about it.

F reedom is more than physically going through the motions of letting go of limits. It means doing the work to deprogram your previously held beliefs about what you've been feared into controlling. Children feel when something is off, and when their parent isn't fully behind something they are doing. They feel the conflict within, and it creates distrust and disconnection.

How do we solve the monumental issues of our times, planting the seeds which could grow into destructive corruption? We stop manipulating children with force and control to meet our needs. We stop insisting that they obey us before they honor themselves, for our fear-based convenience and selfishness. Behavior modification as a focus of parenting is an embarrassing legacy.

The days of rule-based, authoritative parenting are coming to an end.

The world is waking up! An potent and evolved approach is becoming more widely accepted. If you want to solve the roots of corruption, stop modeling an outdated paradigm of power-reigning.

Think deeply about the repercussions in using force and control over those who will lead our future. Are we creating a future that will repeat the horrors of history, or are we cultivating evolved-connectedness, compassion, and kindness?

Parents of babies and young children; Nothing can take the place of nurturing your children at night, in your own arms. There are no blankets, dolls, or teddy bears with heartbeats, that will ever replace you. Surrender to your children's needs, and stop thinking that the goal of parenting is ease, obedience, and convenience.

Go to bed earlier, by your children's side. If your children need you to fall asleep with them, do so with love and devotion. Watch a movie in bed together, read books, and cuddle. Nurse them, tickle their backs, hold their hands, look into their eyes, and smile while you touch their tiny faces. Connect, and meet their physical and emotional needs while they have them – because before you know it, you'll look back in such joy at this time in their lives, and wish for it all back again.

Your children are designed to be dependent. When you meet their natural, dependent needs while they have them, they will be more independent later. This is how it's designed to work!

True freedom and peace comes from ignoring the cultural influences attempting to train you into distancing yourself from your children. Be a parenting rebel, and ignore the voices telling you that being responsive and loving to your child will damage them.

Humans are born wired for freedom. To expect a young child to put your needs before their own innate needs is not only unrealistic, but it is cruel and unjust. Stop demanding obedience. Stop trying to modify their behavior. Stop trying to control them to meet your needs. Step up, and meet your own needs instead of forcing your children to do so. Model this vital life skill. Take responsibility to help them meet their individual needs, as well. Value their needs as much as your own.

The idea of quitting something doesn't exist in our lives, because a child will complete as much as they want of a topic until they are personally satisfied. When they've gained the knowledge, or information, that meets their own needs, they move on. Our children's work doesn't have to be completed according to someone else's standards.

Unschooled kids can go as far as they can understand, or desire. This aspect of natural learning is different than in a forced learning situation, where children are not only made to finish things, but are also graded on how well they do. The focus when it comes to learning, is not on content, but on compliance and obedience.

We respect our children on their own paths in what they want to know in life. Radical Unschooling is focused on trust, freedom, and the belief that humans learn best when they are internally motivated. When children are driven by their own desires, they learn what they need to, and it will not be according to someone else's idea of what is best for them. Learning is pleasurable when it isn't forced.

We live in a Universe where things aren't happening *to* us, they are happening *for* us. Personal growth and evolution can only happen when we learn to be grateful for each and every opportunity to let go of what doesn't serve us anymore.

We can heal when we take responsibility for our lives, without blame. When we unconditionally love others, we allow them to choose their own life, and we set them free.

It is completely unnecessary to create arbitrary limits, and artificial consequences, and wield power over our children, to teach them that there are consequences in the world. In fact, doing so will create such confusion and frustration within them, that they will be at a great disadvantage in life.

Resentment builds towards adults who are supposed to love them, but are instead being cruel and unjust, all for the sake of teaching a lesson they would learn naturally, through living life by our side. There are real-life limits and natural consequences all around us. Our children experience them with us, and through our experiences.

It is unnecessary and damaging to create them artificially in the home, when time spent controlling children could be time connecting with them.

Through discussion and modeling, our children have the benefit of a rock solid foundation of love, support, and trust with us as parents. This is what is severely lacking in the authoritarian paradigm of parenting, which puts children raised this way at a great disadvantage in life. Loving parents never need to be mean to their children to prepare them for the real world. When living in partnership, children learn authentically without cruelty and hypocrisy as the backdrop of their upbringing.

Children make good choices for themselves when supported by a connected and loving parent, who doesn't use their child's freedom as a tool to control them. When children trust their parents, they believe them when they give them information. When there is no power-struggle, children know there is no ulterior motive by a parent. True connection and trust are the foundations of the relationship.

Whom a parent punishes, threatens, limits, and controls their children, all issues center around fear as the backdrop. Children will make choices that aren't healthy or balanced in an attempt to grasp at some sense of freedom in their lives. This is a natural, instinctual drive to be free that will override all else. This becomes the driving force within a child, coming before health, balance, and wellness.

Somehow, in the evolution of humanity, we lost our way. We were told that only bad will come as the result of giving our children an abundant life. Those who were used as the example of this idea seemed to have bad results because of giving to their children.

However, the examples were set for us by those who didn't give true, compassionate, connection-based, love to their children. Instead, they replaced presence with presents. They bought their kids things when they couldn't be there; replacing themselves with material things, in their child's desperate need for connection.

When a parent tries to buy their child's love, it is space and time apart from their child that they are really buying. The child is confused by this dynamic, and learns that love isn't an emotional feeling, it is a material experience.

The warping of the human condition (and the cycle of dysfunction) begins when a parent does this. The concept of giving to our children is observed and judged through this common, dysfunctional intention.

Parents then become fearful of giving their children an abundant life. Children lose out on connection, presence, and the tools they desire for joy, expansion, and learning.

We live in an abundant world, and parents don't have to deliberately deprive their children in order to teach them that life is hard, and they can't always have everything they want.

Children will learn this naturally through discussions about finances, and by observing how we deal with money. Many parents do not talk about money, bills, or finances with their children. I feel they are missing a great opportunity for children to learn in a real-life context about how money works; how to save towards a common goal; and how to give to others, generously.

G iving in presence, instead of in place of your presence, should be the goal when giving to your children.

Authoritarian parents usually deny this fact, claiming that fear and control are their biggest tools to ensure their child's safety and health. They feel that their children can't be trusted, but they have never tried a more respectful, peaceful way. They scream *neglectful* and *lazy* to parents who are patient enough to not let fear control them.

These parents were probably never trusted as children, themselves, so they have no idea what it feels like. They are sadly mistaken, and the warping of the human condition (as a result of such tactics) take a lifetime to recover from - if ever.

Know that there is no way to live a peaceful parenting life with your children, without judgment from others. You will be ridiculed. You will be accused. You will be misunderstood. You will be called a *bad parent*. Just know that I, for one, will always have your back.

You are never alone on this journey. Hold your head high knowing that you are a pioneer, paving the way for future generations. Keep on shining your light for others. It will be accepted, in time.

When you give to your children abundantly, from a place of pure love, they learn generosity and kindness. When you give to your children from a place of guilt or fear, children learn to buy love. This is an important distinction between two intentions in giving, and is one reason why people believe that giving to children will 'spoil' them.

When a parent doesn't know how to give love freely, they use things outside of themselves to replace loving, authentic connection. The results are the 'spoiling' of children, when the intention isn't pure, and from the heart.

Education is not the goal of Unschooling. Our goal is family connection, and pursuing our interests together. Children do get an education as a side effect of living a rich, full, abundant life together, but education is never the main goal before what really matters.

Our home is filled with exciting, fun things to do, like music, art, games, and crafts. Our kitchen cabinets are full of ingredients for cooking and for experiments. Our library overflows with interesting reading material, informative magazines, intriguing games, and puzzles. Our home certainly doesn't look like a home in *Better Homes and Gardens*

Magazine. Instead of viewing our home as a museum for our things, we view is as a workshop for our interests.

W hen adults don't trust children, children don't trust children. Having *frenemies* isn't healthy. Gossiping and backstabbing does not come naturally to young people. It is learned behavior.

W hen kids live controlled lives with punishments and fear as the backdrop, they learn to not trust anyone. When parents are living dysfunctionality, the stage is set for inauthentic, confusing, and unhealthy relationships for the child. Trust yourself. Trust children. It will change the world!

C hildren are the most discriminated against people in our culture today. Much of the damage that many of us are healing from is directly related to how we were raised and treated in our lives, growing up.

As children, we were controlled and abused, even if we weren't aware of it. Control and abuse may have been all that the adults in our lives knew, because it was how they too, were raised. There is a better way – a kinder way – to be with children, which enables them the freedom to live with the joy and confidence that they were naturally born with.

We were raised in an era where the parental role was focused on obedience and control. As children, we were trained to believe that life is about taking orders, which, in essence, only met the needs of the adults in our lives.

Children learn what they live. Being raised in an authoritarian paradigm, children learn that forcing others to meet their needs is what life is all about. This creates a cycle of narcissism that our culture actually blames on a parent not being controlling enough!

Parents today are doing the best they can with what they know. Yet, many feel empty, and wonder why their children don't want to be around them.

We hear words like *rebellion,* and chalk it up to normalcy, but what if there was nothing to rebel against?

What if we lived the respect for our children we demand they have for us?

What if we could recognize that punishments model meanness, and that, through using power to control another person, we are teaching them to do the same?

It is though loving, kindness, and understanding that our children learn love and peace, and, in turn, reflect this back to the world.

My children's interests and passions are something that I respect as an extension of who they are. I do not judge one interest as having more value in their lives over another. I see the learning in all that my kids do.

School subjects are what most of us were brainwashed to believe were most important to focus on. I believe that the most important subject in my child's life is whatever they happen to interested in at the moment.

My child's interest is the nucleus of their learning at any given moment. So much branches off from a passionate interest.

Although we don't live life broken down into subjects, if you were to view their interests with a *school filter*, you would see that, through pursuing a passion, we touch on all of the traditional school subjects. Science, math, English, History, and geography, are all naturally covered as a side affect of delving into one's interests, thoroughly.

We live life holistically, driven by our passions. In doing so, our children get an education which is perfectly catered to who they are as individuals, without ever needing to force them into doing anything they don't want to do. Children can, and do, learn in complete freedom, much to the surprise of a culture that has been brainwashed into believing otherwise.

You don't see animals in the wild feeling insecure, or living with low self-esteem. It isn't something that needs to be instilled in children, unless they are robbed of it, through living a life where others value obedience and conformity over a child's own needs and desires.

You are a unique and powerful individual. When you feel like you don't fit in anywhere, be proud that you don't. I'm certainly grateful that I don't!

You have great purpose. Feeling like you are alone in this world, that you are unloved, or that no one likes you, is all an illusion. It's your mind messing with you, trying to make sense of your purpose.

You will find your purpose if you can step back from the pain, silence your mind, and allow the Universe to speak through you, and guide you.

Not fitting in is the first step in you being part of changing the world.

Love and trust are the most overlooked aspects of true learning for a child. It is not the latest technique, or a sneaky tool that a parent needs to grasp in order to manipulate a child to learn something new. Trusting children to learn what they need to, with our loving facilitation and support, takes courage, trust, and most importantly, respect.

You are someone's enemy. You are someone's greatest joy. You are someone's reason for living, and another's reason for crying. Your role in this life is to embrace it all, to allow yourself to grow, and change, and evolve, and to fulfil your purpose and destiny.

These are such important words to remember. We are here for the true human experience. All of the emotions and experiences we have, will help build who we desire to become. It is all essential in our personal evolution.

People will love you, and some will hate you. Some will understand you, and some will never get who you are, or why you've made the choices you have. Embrace it all, and stop trying to control others' perspective (or opinions) of you.

Times are changing. Consciousness is evolving. The old paradigm of parenting has shown us (again and again) that it simply *does not work*.

Parenting (as we once knew it) is outdated and damaging. In time, we will look back on the past as a shameful time in human history, and we will wonder how it went on for so long. When we collectively evolve enough to give children the rights and respect that they so deserve, human relationships will step into a new era of richness we've never experienced before.

Many of us were told that the adults in our lives controlled us *because* they loved us. We were told that children whose parents didn't treat them that way, weren't loved. We began to form the belief that *control* is how we express *love* to someone else. We had to believe this as children! It was a survival mechanism. But something within us has always known this idea is wrong. However, many learned to silence that inner-voice, and have for so long, that they began disconnecting from the truth it shared.

When our inner-voice becomes a soft whisper, it's easier to ignore it, and 'cope' with the pain in life.

Self-doubt, and distrust of one's inner-voice, is a sad, but very real, side-effect of control.

None of my children ever slept in a crib. Not even for one night! I've co-slept with all of them, and they are all healthy, independent humans today.

Be who you are, fully!

Learn from it all.

Grow in ways you never thought possible.

Trust your path, and your journey.

∼

Cradle the inner child that resides in your soul.

∼

Embrace YOU!

∼

Be compassionate and empathetic.

∼

LOVE and FORGIVE.

∼

Most of all...
Trust Yourself.

∼

ALSO BY DAYNA MARTIN